EXPLORING JUDAISM:
A RECONSTRUCTIONIST APPROACH

EXPLORING JUDAISM

A RECONSTRUCTIONIST APPROACH

Rebecca T. Alpert
and
Jacob J. Staub

THE RECONSTRUCTIONIST PRESS
Wyncote, Pennsylvania
1988

Library of Congress Number: 85-62282

International Standard Book Numbers:
0-935457-00-3 (paperback)
0-935457-01-1 (clothbound)

Second Printing, 1988

Cover by Nina Gaelen
Book design by Alvin Schultzberg

Back cover photos by Rosalyn Handel and Jerry Miller

Published by
The Reconstructionist Press
Church Road and Greenwood Avenue
Wyncote, Pennsylvania 19095

Printed in the United States of America

In Honor of

Miriam and W. Maxwell Passerman

*Whose Grant Has Made Possible the Publication
of this
Introduction to Reconstructionist Judaism*

Gifts from the following people made the printing of this edition possible:

Fred and Linda Greenberg
Don and Betsy Landis
Aaron and Marjorie Ziegelman

TABLE OF CONTENTS

ACKNOWLEDGEMENTS

Writing a book is often pictured as a solitary enterprise. In fact, the opposite was true for us. This book is an exercise in collaboration. We begin by acknowledging each other; it is no exaggeration to say that we found working together to be an amazing experience of discovering how easily two can speak with one voice.

It is also our happy task to acknowledge all those who worked with us, enabling us to have this privilege: our benefactors, Miriam and Maxwell Passerman, who provided the material resources that made this project possible; our editor and muse, David Teutsch, who with his boundless energies and creativity sustained and cajoled us each step of the way; the FRCH Publications Committee, composed of Mordecai Lewittes, Charles Lieber, Henry Feingold, Joy Levitt, and Richard Hirsh, who gave us guidance and direction; our readers Ira Eisenstein, Arthur Green, and Jeffrey Schein, who gave us their helpful and persuasive suggestions; our typist, Sharon Polsky, whose efficiency, good humor, and excellence never failed; the members of the Reconstructionist community, who live what we have written about in these pages; and our families, Barbara, Leah, and Andrew Staub, and Joel, Lynn, and Avram Alpert, who nurtured us with their patient love.

The writing of the book has also been collaborative in another important way. We have tried to present a Reconstructionist perspective that reasonably represents the various outlooks included today in the Reconstructionist movement. As we hope will remain clear throughout the chapters that follow, no one can speak for all Reconstructionists. This is a healthy consequence of the movement's ideology, which encourages individual people and communities to confront Jewish civilization and to come to terms with its various aspects. Thus, we interacted not only with each other, but with the various voices in the movement. We tried to speak for ourselves and for others as well. The results are not to be taken as the official viewpoint of the movement; ultimately, they represent our views alone. We do hope, however, that they offer the reader a sense of the Reconstructionist perspective.

Wyncote, Pennsylvania   Rebecca T. Alpert
24 Nisan 5745—15 April 1985   Jacob J. Staub

iii

PREFACE

In the last decade, the Reconstructionist movement has enjoyed unprecedented growth. The number of affiliated congregations and
havurot doubled from 1980 to 1985 alone, and the new groups include a generation of American Jews who had never before associated with the movement. The growth of the Reconstructionist Rabbinical College, founded in 1968, has provided North American Jews
with a new generation of leaders who have a different concept of the
rabbinate, the synagogue, and the meaning of Jewish life. As a consequence, the graduates of the RRC find themselves in great demand.
The movement has pioneered in such matters as developing birth
rituals for girls, outreach to intermarried couples, and synthesizing
contemporary and traditional forms of worship. Thousands of people across the North American continent who had been disillusioned
with the Jewish community and alienated from the Jewish tradition
are now active and committed Jews because of their involvement
with Reconstructionism. Thus Reconstructionism has enabled Jews
to find new ways to express what it means to be a Jew today.

In spite of all these facts, Reconstructionism is barely recognized
by American Jewry as the fourth Jewish movement, and for many, remains a footnoted afterthought when American Judaism is described.
Millions of North American Jews have never even heard the term. A
young movement only just beginning to acquire institutional resources like those of the other movements, Reconstructionist Judaism is still relatively unknown. This book is being written to remedy
that circumstance.

What is a Reconstructionist? All those associated with the movement are accustomed to the question and to the frustration of not being able to answer it "on one foot," in a simple declarative sentence.

"Reconstructionist Jews are willing to question conventional
answers and keep open minds. They believe that a Jew need not and
ought not sacrifice intellectual integrity for the sake of his/her Jewish
identity."

"Reconstructionists are Jews who take the Jewish tradition seriously and live Jewish lives even though they don't believe in the
divine, supernatural origin of the Torah."

"Reconstructionists believe that, just as Jewish civilization has adapted to new circumstances throughout Jewish history, so must it adapt to late twentieth-century North American society."

"Reconstructionists tend to conduct more intimate worship services in which everyone is involved and the rabbi—if there is one—does not dominate."

"One of the ways that Reconstructionists tend to express their Jewish commitments is through social and political action."

Though each of these statements is accurate, none is a fair and comprehensive one-sentence definition. We can find out more by asking a different question. A better question than "What is a Reconstructionist?" is "How do Reconstructionists approach living as Jews?" We ask this question because we assume that what matters about Judaism is how we live it every day. Being Jewish affects our total being—thoughts and feelings, behaviors and relationships, our stance in the world community. This book describes the Reconstructionist approach to being Jewish.

One does not become a Reconstructionist simply by joining a Reconstructionist synagogue or by paying dues to a national organization. Our name itself indicates *active participation* in a shared process. No mere passive adjective describing a "type" of Judaism, our name says that each of us engages in just that—the reconstruction of Jewish life and tradition to integrate it with the particular lifestyle that each of us chooses. The Reconstructionist community is not a body of synagogues and rabbis that others merely support. It is rather a community in the full sense of the term, in which no one's duty may be done vicariously by others. It is a community of Jews who commit themselves to ongoing study, to discussion of issues, and to a life of intelligent decision making.

Jews can and do take different approaches to Jewish life. To some extent, our differences may be understood by looking at the names we call ourselves. Clearly, those who approach Judaism as "traditionalist" or "conservative" are looking to preserve and express those values and behaviors which they see as *inherently meaningful* and *permanently present* in Judaism. Those who describe themselves as "reformers" emphasize making changes and adapting traditions to bring Judaism into consonance with the world in which we live.

Those who seek to reconstruct, on the other hand, approach the issue of Jewish life in a radically different manner. The term "reconstruct" involves two clear assumptions. First, that each generation prior to our own played a role in constructing the Judaism which is now ours. Thus, traditional meanings have changed over time; they have not always been conserved in the past and certainly should not be seen as permanent today. Reconstructionists use the foundation and building blocks they have inherited from the past, reordering and adding to them so that they fit the needs, values, and tastes of this generation, without altering them in ways that would make them unrecognizable or sap their richness.

Second, that the basic structures of Jewish life are in need of serious rethinking. These include such institutional structures as the Jewish community and the synagogue, with special reference to the quality of interpersonal relationships and value orientations that exist within them. Reconstruction also applies to the organized Jewish community as a whole, including the nature of diaspora Jewry's all-important relationship to the State of Israel and the centers of Jewish creativity there. It applies to the basic intellectual structures of Jewish life as well as to the social ones—to the way we think about God, to traditional religious language, to prayer, and to the role of the Jewish people in history.

In Hebrew, the term given to Reconstructionism is "*shikkum hayahadut.*" *Shikkum* is a term often used to refer to the reconstruction of physical buildings. The metaphor is a good one. Judaism, to Reconstructionists, is a spiritual and physical structure, in need of constant revitalization, reevaluation, repair or, if you will, reconstruction.

How this approach has been used by Jews who call themselves Reconstructionists will be spelled out in the pages that follow. In a world changing ever more quickly, it becomes increasingly important to make the effort to think through carefully how we will reconstruct Judaism in every generation. That will help us to fulfill our Jewish lives and pass on a thriving Jewish culture to our children. Thus, being a Reconstructionist means being constantly involved in exploring one's Jewishness. We do this not only for ourselves. The approach that we take, which has made it possible for us to live meaningful lives as Jews today, provides an example to others. So many Jews who are dissatisfied with the Jewish institutions in which they were raised are at the same time searching for meaning, looking for a place to call home. A reconstructed Judaism may in fact be such a place.

That place would not exist within Jewish life were it not for the teachings of one great man, Rabbi Mordecai M. Kaplan (1881–1983).

Kaplan adopted the term "reconstruction" and articulated a program for its implementation. It is Kaplan's conceptual framework which provides the blueprint for this volume.

Kaplan set the standard for us: to reconstruct. It is up to us to study the program he created for the reconstruction of Judaism in his generation, and then to build upon it for our own. That is how we understand his mandate and legacy to us.

CHAPTER ONE

THE CREATION OF AN AMERICAN JUDAISM

The Choice to be Jewish

Jews have not always been able to choose whether or not to identify with the Jewish people. That choice has been available for less than two hundred years. Prior to the modern era, the Jewish community was granted complete jurisdiction over its members by outside governing authorities. Jewish law was the only law. Jewish education was the only education available. The only social services were Jewish. Jews lived in a *kehillah*—an organic Jewish community from which the only exit was apostasy. Converting to Christianity or Islam was, for most Jews, an unimaginable option. The wide cultural gap between the Jews and their neighbors in most periods of Jewish history made social integration difficult. Moreover, Jews believed in the divine origin of the Torah and their election by God, just as Muslims and Christians made similar, contradictory claims.

Thus, while the vast majority of Jews alive today have the ability at any time to abandon all connections with the Jewish people and our tradition without adopting another religious affiliation, this revolutionary circumstance is relatively new. It is a consequence of one of the fundamental aspects of the modern nation-state, which extends the rights and responsibilities of citizenship to individuals, but not to groups. In the past, the Jewish community had to strike a bargain with the ruling monarch—for example, promising a certain number of tax dollars in return for the right to live autonomously under Jewish law. The modern state, by contrast, normally does not tolerate autonomous subgroups, but rather demands the individual citizen's complete political allegiance.

To be sure, one can look back into Jewish history and see periods during which individual Jews asked daring questions and had a great deal of freedom. But those daring questions were about *how* to be part of the Jewish community. The radical break which occurred with the beginning of modernity has afforded Jews the choice of *whether* to remain in the Jewish community at all.

Such is the mixed blessing of the "emancipation" of the Jewish people, which commenced at the end of the eighteenth century.

1

While Jews rejoiced at the equal rights which they were accorded (believing naively that social and political integration would bring an end to anti-Semitism), many rabbis anxiously lamented the new freedom of the individual Jew, who was now at liberty to ignore rabbinic pronouncements.

But there is more. It was not only the political realities that changed. The prevailing world view underwent a radical transformation as well. In the past, Jews had shared with Muslims and Christians common beliefs in God, in sacred scripture, in reward and punishment, in life after death. They had differed on the details while agreeing on the principles. Now, the newly emancipated Jew entered societies in Western Europe and North America in which the prevailing ideologies were influenced by humanism and by the scientific revolution. People cared more about human potentialities than about God's attributes; more about happiness in this life than heavenly reward; more about investigating the causes of natural phenomena than about attributing them to God's will. Christian culture had already been adjusting to these questions for several centuries, since the Renaissance and Protestant Reformation. By contrast, Jews were thrust out of their ghettoized existence abruptly, without time to modernize. The initial impulse of many of them was to discard Judaism entirely.

Finally, Jews—especially in North America—were faced with a modern political ideology which beckoned all citizens to become one nation under God, to abandon their foreign baggage and embrace fully a new, unprecedented society in which everyone was equal. In this context, Jewish commitments seemed not only obstructively separatist but antiquated as well. It is an integrated person indeed who can fully embrace the universal human family without abandoning Jewish allegiances.

Much of the history of Judaism in the modern era can be seen as a struggle between opposing forces. On the one hand, social, political, and ideological forces have drawn Jews away from Judaism, while, on the other, committed Jews have devoted themselves to the task of persuading other Jews to remain Jewish. Out of our European heritage came Reform, Conservative, Orthodox, Zionist, Yiddishist, and other ethnic/cultural and philosophical approaches to the question, all of which have been transplanted in one way or another to the Western hemisphere.

Perhaps the only truly indigenous attempt to solve the problem of modernity for American Jewry is the philosophy of Mordecai Kaplan. How Kaplan came to focus on an American response to the modern challenge becomes clear when we look at his life in the context of American and Jewish history.

The Life and Thought of Mordecai M. Kaplan

Kaplan was born in Lithuania in 1881. At the age of nine he came to America when his father, an Orthodox rabbi, was called to these shores to become the assistant to Rabbi Jacob Joseph. Rabbi Joseph was serving at the time as "Chief Rabbi of New York." This attempt by Eastern European Jews to set up a community cohesive enough to have a chief rabbi indicates that there were Jews who wished to establish the traditional Jewish communal structure in America, so that Jewish identity would not be eroded by modernity. But the vast majority of Jews saw America as a place where they could shed much of their Jewishness.

In his youth, Kaplan was sheltered from Jews who rejected Judaism altogether. He was influenced, however, by people with new approaches to the Jewish tradition. He was exposed at an early age to people like Arnold Ehrlich, a scholar of the Bible who asked radical questions about divine authorship. He was sent to study at the fledgling Jewish Theological Seminary of America. Unlike the traditional yeshiva which sought to strengthen Jewish separation, the Seminary was organized to "Americanize" Eastern European Jews while immersing them in Jewish study.

Kaplan also attended Columbia University, becoming exposed to the teachings of modern American thought. He studied philosophy, sociology, and anthropology, and began to develop a broad view of human culture.

Although these new ideas challenged the traditional Jewish world view, for Kaplan they also provided the reason for remaining Jewish. He applied the theories he learned to describing how Judaism could function in the modern world. Kaplan took it as his challenge to prove that being Jewish is an exemplary way of being human, that Judaism should be understood in light of the latest theories and knowledge of human culture. For Kaplan, bringing contemporary insights to the understanding of Judaism results in living a rich life as an American *and* as a Jew, without the need to forsake either culture for the other.

Kaplan spent many years working out his theories. Although he maintained an ongoing position as a faculty member and administrator at the Jewish Theological Seminary until his retirement in 1963, that institution did not provide a setting where Kaplan's program for Judaism could be carried out. He needed to find a community of Jews who were interested in working on the experiment in Jewish living with him. A founder in 1912 of the Orthodox Young Israel movement, and in 1913, along with Solomon Schechter, of the Conservative United Synagogue, he found neither fully responsive to the American Jewish challenge.

In 1922, Kaplan founded the Society for the Advancement of Judaism (SAJ), a synagogue in New York City. He had been much discouraged by his prior experiences with congregations—so much so that he had considered seriously abandoning the rabbinate to become an insurance salesman. With the establishment of the SAJ, however, Kaplan was free to propound his ideas and enter into a dialogue about them with a group of people open to his views. Because of his experiences at the SAJ, he was able to write and bring his ideas to a wider audience. In 1934, at age 53, Kaplan published his first major work, *Judaism as a Civilization*, which is considered his magnum opus. Many other works followed. With the founding of the Jewish Reconstructionist Foundation in 1940, he achieved an international platform which stood unequivocally for the kind of approach Kaplan advocated.

His books, especially *Judaism as a Civilization*, his magazine— the *SAJ Review*, later renamed the *Reconstructionist*—his daring liturgical innovations, his involvement in restructuring Jewish communal and educational institutions, and his activism on behalf of women's religious equality were his main contributions to Jewish thought and to the debate on why and how to be a Jew in modern America.

Kaplan drew his followers from the ever-expanding population of the SAJ, and from the many people around the country who heard him lecture and teach. But it was as a teacher of rabbis at the Jewish Theological Seminary that his reputation was established. While many of his students did not identify as his disciples, they nevertheless were influenced by him in subtle and profound ways, so that it is not an exaggeration to state that Kaplan changed the nature of American Judaism in the 1930s and 1940s.

Some of the rabbis he trained became ardent followers of Kaplan. They urged Kaplan to spread his message, and to start a movement in Jewish life with institutions to promote his ideas. The leader among them was Ira Eisenstein, who also married Kaplan's eldest daughter, Judith. It was Eisenstein who formally assumed the leadership of the Reconstructionist movement. He wrote books which interpreted Kaplan's teachings and became the editor of the *Reconstructionist* magazine. He also was primarily responsible for establishing key institutions of Reconstructionist life—the Federation of Reconstructionist Congregations and Havurot in 1954, and the Reconstructionist Rabbinical College in 1968.

As the institutions of Reconstructionism grew and developed, Kaplan's philosophy in all its specifics remained at the core of Reconstructionist ideology. For several decades, the Reconstructionist movement was based exclusively on his teachings. However, now that both the Federation of Reconstructionist Congregations and Havurot, and the Reconstructionist Rabbinical College are growing and thriving, the majority of Reconstructionists are no longer drawn from those personally devoted to Kaplan and the *specific* formulations of his ideas. Kaplan's teachings are viewed not as the end of the story, but as the beginning.

Kaplan set the agenda, pinpointing those areas of Jewish life which need reconstruction if we are to meet the challenge of remaining Jewish in the modern world. But if we are to remain true to Kaplan's teachings, we must take cognizance of the fact that the world in which he lived and wrote is vastly different from our own.

Kaplan's life was very much influenced by the burgeoning wisdom available from the social sciences. Those new understandings of human life which Kaplan unreservedly accepted led him to various conclusions about what it might mean to be Jewish. Today we draw on a much wider range of academic disciplines. Indeed, even the discipline of sociology, on which he relied, has developed in unanticipated ways. At the same time, we are more willing to question the authority and objectivity of social scientific research.

Kaplan's thinking assumed that the values embodied in American society—values like liberty and democracy—are the culmination of the progress of human civilization. Today, we tend to be less certain that all aspects of American society are the ideals toward which every civilization ought to aspire, and we tend to put increased emphasis on non-American aspects of the Jewish tradition. Thus, our sense of the proper balance between the two is different from his.

In Kaplan's day, the predominant world view exalted the impersonal approach of the scientist and assumed that rational beings would use their minds together to create a better world. Today, living after Auschwitz and under the threat of nuclear holocaust, some of us question more vigorously the extent of our capabilities to bring about a better world by using politics and technology to achieve the good and the true. We no longer revere technology; we use it while recognizing it as a tool to be regarded cautiously.

Kaplan lived in an era when nationalism was perceived to be a force for good. Today, some of us question the power of nation-states to do more than war against one another.

In Kaplan's generation, intellectuals were involved in a debate about theism and atheism. Today, existentialism has replaced empiricism as the frame of reference, so that most thoughtful Jews do not struggle with the question, "Does God exist?", but rather with the question, "What is the truth-value of inner experience and religious consciousness?" There is thus a new focus on the cultivation of inwardness. With the resolution of the question about the literal, supernaturalistic picture of God, we seek to discover ways to sense and manifest the divine presence in our lives.

Finally, since the Second World War, we live much more in a global village in which East and West are no longer so separate. Some of the influence of Eastern culture and religion has been faddish, but not all. Whereas Kaplan was working in Western categories, Jews today also must deal with the challenge of Eastern-style religious consciousness.

In order to be faithful Reconstructionists, we must build our reconstruction of Judaism on our own world view. Yet Kaplan's thnking is our cornerstone and our challenge.

The task undertaken below is to describe Kaplan's program for reconstructing American Judaism, to look at that program through contemporary eyes, and to validate, augment, or reconstruct elements which need to be presented today in a different light. Thus this book should chart a way of being Jewish that meets decisively the challenge of living as a Jew today.

CHAPTER TWO

AN EVOLVING RELIGIOUS CIVILIZATION

Searching for a Definition

What modernity gave to the individual Jew in terms of rights and identity, it took away from the Jews as a group. No longer would the community, the *kehillah*, function as an all-embracing Jewish society that provided for the individual's social, religious, economic, and political needs. With the elimination of the *kehillah*, the community lost much of its ability to preserve group identity. The resulting benefits were enormous, both to Jews *as individuals*, and to general society, in terms of the contributions of individual Jews. One need only mention Freud and Einstein in this context to highlight the point. But the loss to the Jews *as a group* was enormous as well, for they no longer possessed an encompassing sense of identity.

Many Jews welcomed the option and rejected identification with the group entirely. But for most, Jewish group identity was still a crucial matter. Attempts were made to redefine Jewish group identity in new terms.

Some sought to define being Jewish as membership in a religion. This brought Judaism into line with Christianity, and made it understandable to those with whom the Jews were now permitted to associate. This definition worked not only for Reform Jews but for the more traditional in Western Europe as well.

Others, chiefly in Eastern Europe, were influenced by modern nationalism, and sought to describe being Jewish as being part of a nationality. They urged Jews to seek a territory in which to live together so that their nation could be like all other nations. This solution to the question of Jewish identity is most often associated with Zionism and the establishment of the State of Israel. But there were also groups of Jews who wished to set up Jewish collectivities in the other lands in which Jews lived.

Still others, influenced by theories about ethnic origins, defined Jewishness as a factor of ethnic identity. They linked Jews by physical characteristics and traits. This definition of Jewry was imposed externally as often as self-defined. It could be negative ("Jews are rich and have large noses"), positive ("Jews are intelligent and make good husbands"), or neutral ("Jews like to eat lox and bagels").

Of course, each of those definitions of being Jewish has some truth to it. There are Jews for whom being Jewish involves religious faith alone, or Israeli citizenship alone, or pride in one's ancestry, and nothing more. What was missing in Kaplan's time was a definition of Judaism broad enough to include *all* of these subgroups, so that Jewish nationalists, Jewish social activists, and Jewish worshippers could articulate the nature of their unity.

Peoplehood

It was the genius of Mordecai Kaplan to capture this sense of Jewish collectivity. He defined Judaism in a way that combined all of these discrete elements for the first time. He simply stated that the Jews are a people. As a people, Jews are interconnected through a common history, experience, and destiny; they are linked together as a group by their shared past, their mutual concern in the present, and their shared future destiny.

Individuals may choose diverse ways to link themselves to the Jewish people, but it is belonging to that people that makes us all Jews. Not only does this definition of Jews as a people link us to our ancestors. It also illustrates that we are but one among the many peoples of the world, an integral part of the human family. While other interpretations of Judaism have sought to describe us as a people apart, Kaplan's definition suggests that we should see ourselves as related to other peoples and equivalent to them.

By redefining Jewishness in terms of belonging rather than believing, Kaplan sought to recapture some of the flavor of Jewish living prior to the modern era. Before the political emancipation of the Jews, a Jewish person acquired Jewish identity by virtue of membership in the community and not just because of theological or political or liturgical commitments. One came to one's Jewishness because one was raised in the Jewish community and culture. Members of the extended family of the people diverged widely in their philosophical, devotional, and even ritual commitments, but as they fought with one another, their Jewishness was not at issue.

The Problems of Belonging

For Kaplan himself, and for his initial audience of first-generation American Jews, this sense of belonging still came naturally. They were in direct touch with parents who had lived in the shtetls (Jewish villages) of East Europe. They spoke Yiddish and had been raised in places like the Lower East Side. Their task was to Americanize—to shed the trappings of Jewish belonging. Many were on the verge of cutting all ties to the Jewish tradition. Thus they were interested in Kaplan's argument that they could *belong* to the Jewish people without necessarily believing or behaving in the traditional manner of their forebears.

Jews today often do not see themselves as part of the Jewish community and do not always experience a sense of identification with the Jewish people as a whole. For them a sense of belonging primarily to the Jewish people is anything but natural. We no longer live in Jewish communities. Our friends, neighbors, and colleagues are not necessarily Jewish, and if they are, their Jewishness is often incidental to our relationship with them. Most of us don't know how to sing the songs of Shabbat, for example, and even those of us who do know them often cannot sing them comfortably, as if it were the natural thing to do at a Friday evening dinner or a Saturday lunch.

Moreover, we have lost our ancestors' sense of oneness with the past. They interpreted the events in their lives as an integral part of a cosmic and providential drama. They had been exiled for their sins, and they awaited messianic redemption in their belief that God would not abandon them. They believed that their souls had been present at Sinai for the giving of the Torah because they belonged to a community whose reason for being was that very event.

We, by contrast, have lost a sense of active memory. Most of us have internalized the modern historian's view of the past. We attempt to understand the experiences of our ancestors in their historical context. It is often difficult for us to imagine that they really believed that God was an active force in their lives and the life of the Jewish people.

Kaplan suggested that an empathic understanding of our past would make it more meaningful in the present. Much of the effort of Reconstructionists is devoted to regaining a oneness with the past, even as we maintain an awareness of the importance of the present. This quest for belonging will be elaborated below, when we describe the Reconstructionist approach to ritual, to historical awareness, and to a contemporary community.

Judaism as a Civilization

Once belonging is established as the essential part of Jewish group self-definition, we must begin to discover the basic characteristics of the group to which we belong. What is Judaism? Kaplan supplied that definition too. Judaism is not merely a religion or a nationality, and it certainly is not a race. Kaplan defined Judaism as the *evolving religious civilization of the Jewish people*. Each of the key words in this definition will be discussed separately to show its full breadth and depth.

Like peoplehood, *civilization* implies a totality. Civilization encompasses all of the elements of group life: art, culture, philosophy, language, law, ethics, celebrations, patterns of eating and dressing, sancta (holy things, times, events, and places). Every group that has ever functioned has included these elements in its group life. Being Jewish, by Kaplan's definition, is in some ways like being Canadian, Greek, Irish, or Native American. One belongs to a group and participates in the life of that group as one's primary way of being in the world. As will be discussed later, one can live in more than one civilization at a time. But there is no question that one must have a primary identification.

Because of the nature of contemporary society, our lives are fragmented into many pieces—family, work, and leisure activities fall into separate compartments. In the process, we lose the sense that our lives are unified wholes. A civilizational definition of Judaism can be of assistance in regaining our self-integration. As individuals, we may need to pursue paths which emphasize different parts of ourselves. If we belong organically to the Jewish civilization, however, we can begin to see ourselves as elements in a greater scheme of things and thus achieve a greater sense of wholeness.

Viewing Judaism as a civilization also enables us to appreciate those elements of Judaism often taken for granted or forgotten. The Jewish arts, for example music, literature, dance, drama, and photography, take on new importance when looking at the totality of Jewish civilization. Kaplan urged that we emphasize these underdeveloped elements. They are the natural expressions of a living civilization and have been ignored for too long. The recent burgeoning of Jewish crafts and art is a welcome revitalization of Jewish civilization.

Finally, the civilizational view leads us to appreciate that each of us has something to contribute to Jewish life, no matter what our talents or interests. Jewish creativity arises in many areas: the arts, cooking, writing, teaching, building, settling arguments, choosing values, playing, dreaming. All of these activities—and more—can be cultivated as part of the civilization of the Jewish people; one's Jewishness need not be measured primarily by synagogue attendance or eating habits.

A Religious Civilization

No two civilizations are identical. Some seem to produce great sculptors, others, intricate systems of social organization. When Kaplan defined Judaism as a civilization, he did not intend to imply that Judaism is substantially identical to all other civilizations. For him, the primary identifying feature of Jewish civilization lies in its religious aspects.

What do we mean by religion? Religion is the search to discover what is ultimately meaningful in life and to find ways of expressing the resulting visions of the ultimate in behaviors and ideas.

Taking his cue from the studies of social scientists, Kaplan understood religion as a group phenomenon rather than as an individual one. Kaplan did not agree with Alfred North Whitehead, who defined religion as what a person does with solitude. Although every individual arrives at his or her own religious vision and finds those elements in religious behavior which enhance his or her own life, this search must take place within the context of a group.

Every group expresses its vision of the ultimate through statements of faith and ritual actions, through sacred stories and traditional customs. Words, narratives, and patterns of behavior all derive their sanctity from their personal connection with an ultimate source of wisdom and power.

In theistic religions, that source is called God, and in Judaism, God manifests divine wisdom in the Torah. Thus, all aspects of a Jew's life can be sanctified because they can be viewed in terms of their divine source and connection: one recites a blessing of gratitude for each kind of food one eats; if one treats one's customers in accordance with the *mitzvot* (commandments), one is a partner with God in the redemption of the universe; when one reads the newspaper, it is with the implicit understanding that current events have a greater meaning and purpose—even if that purpose eludes us. In sum, a religion is the aspect of a culture with which we structure reality, separating the significant from the insignificant, interpreting the apparently chaotic events of our lives in a meaningful and orderly way.

Of course, the traditional Jew believes that all of the commandments, articles of faith, and rituals are literally God-given. Taking his cue from modern historians and social scientists, Kaplan understood that *every people* makes such a claim for the religious aspect of its civilization. For most of us, it is more accurate and more helpful to understand the religion of the Jewish people as the expression of our people's highest values and most profound wisdom, without claiming that our religion is exactly identical with the will and wisdom of a perfect God. In other words, what a generation hears God say tells us at least as much about the problems and values of that generation as about God. As social situations and moral values change, so do human interpretations of God and the regulations of *halakhah* (Jewish law).

One of the distinctive characteristics of Jewish civilization is the way in which religion is infused in elements of culture—food, clothing, language, literature, law—which are not usually associated with the Western definition of religion. In Europe, Christianity was superimposed upon particular national cultures, so that there was a clear distinction between the sacred and profane aspects of one's life. That tendency is even more pronounced in America, where the separation of religion and secular life, of church and state, is elevated to a constitutional principle. Jewish civilization, by contrast, is a religious civilization—its language is a sacred one, its meals have ultimate significance, and there is not a similar distinction between synagogue and marketplace.

Furthermore, the great ideas that Judaism has contributed to human understanding have been expressed in religious terms. The social concepts and moral values that have shaped much of Western civilization are suggested in the Ten Commandments and made explicit in the great religious literature of the Jewish people—the Bible, the Talmud, the collections of Midrash, the Siddur. Religion was not divorced from life in the daily activities of the Jewish people. Perhaps the impact of these ideas, which have so greatly influenced Western civilization for several thousand years, lies in the way they bring religious values to daily living.

For most Jews today, even if religion is central to the Jewish perspective, it is not all-encompassing. This is the case because of the role of religion in contemporary society, where religion commonly is restricted to those aspects of life that are synagogue/church related and that involve an explicit profession of faith in God. More than ever before, today one can live a Jewish life and not perceive it as "religious" in any way. One can decide to participate in and observe Jewish customs and rites without attaching ultimate meanings to them. For example, it is possible to keep a kosher home for the purpose of maintaining a link to the Jewish collectivity, or because one's family did, or because one wants any Jew to be comfortable eating in one's home, or because one finds kashrut aesthetic—without ever having a sense of kashrut as a religious observance. One can be fluent in Hebrew and use it daily as a teacher, interpreter, or flight attendant for El Al Airlines, without attaching any explicitly religious meaning to the language. Without examining the religious significance of the holiday, one can light Hanukah candles every year as a way to express one's Jewish identity, while most of America expresses its Christian identity.

Many people would be tempted to dismiss such secularization of Jewish custom as inappropriate and inauthentic. Certainly, the traditionalists among us affirm unremittingly that Jewish civilization must remain as halakhically and supernaturally oriented as it was in the past. Reconstructionists, by contrast, believe that our civilization must be reconstructed to adapt to the unprecedented circumstances of our era. In an era in which traditional beliefs about God and miracles and providence are called into question, it is legitimate to be a cultural Jew who both identifies with Jewish civilization and remains uncomfortable with its inherited religious strand. The secular Jews who express their Jewishness by writing Yiddish stories, eating latkes, making aliyah to live on a secular kibbutz where Jewish tradition is disregarded, doing Israeli dancing, or making an annual contribution to the UJA, should not be excluded from Jewish life because they refuse to see themselves as religious.

Reconstructionists would argue nonetheless that Jews who disavow the central religious aspect of Jewish civilization are disowning the most enriching and profound parts of the tradition they inherit. It is true that the religious insights of our ancestors are phrased in supernaturalistic terms and values that no longer speak to us. But when the traditional rationales for beliefs and practices lose their meaning, Jews can and should revalue them to express our own most exalted values—thus continuing the evolution of Judaism. This will be discussed at greater length below when we address ritual observance directly. Nevertheless, defining Judaism as a "religious civilization," rather than as a "religion," leaves room for secularist perspectives without mistaking the vital role that religion has played and continues to play in the lives of Jews.

The Evolution of Jewish Civilization

The last element of the definition suggests that Judaism is an *evolving* civilization. At first glance this appears obvious. Don't all civilizations evolve, change, grow, and decline? From the vantage point of the historian, this clearly would be the case. Looking at the question from the perspective of traditional Judaism, however, the idea that Judaism is evolving presents serious problems. Rabbinic Judaism was founded on the supposition of the fundamental immutability of the Torah, God's word. True, we have had scholars in every generation to interpret Torah, but only to extract Torah's unchanging meaning as it applies to the changed social situation of each generation. Furthermore, from the viewpoint of traditional Judaism, the latitude of interpretation as well as the ability of the interpreters grows weaker in time as we move farther and farther away from the event at Sinai.

In our definition of Judaism as evolving, Reconstructionists take fundamental issue with this perspective. For us, Judaism has been created by Jews over the course of our history. Judaism necessarily has evolved because all of human culture evolves and adapts to changing historical circumstances. It is inaccurate to claim that the rituals and beliefs of contemporary Orthodox Jews date back to Sinai. In every era, our ancestors interacted with neighboring cultures and reinterpreted laws in accordance with the needs and values of the times. The creation story in Genesis resembles Babylonian stories from the same period; the Ten Commandments, Hittite treaties; the Pesaḥ seder, a Roman feast; the dress of Ḥasidim, the garb of eighteenth-century Polish nobles. Slavery was prohibited rather late in Jewish history, and the bar mitzvah ceremony introduced even later.

The term "evolution" is sometimes understood as implying that Jewish civilization has progressed steadily from the time of our primitive ancestors to our own era, in which our understanding of nature is more accurate than ever before and our ethical sensibilities are more elevated than ever before. Such views are a form of modernistic triumphalism.

That is *not* the intention of our use of the term "evolution." In the evolution of species, one form survives because it is better adapted to new environmental conditions. It is not superior except with reference to the current conditions in which it lives. Similarly, we advocate an evolution of Jewish civilization which continually adapts to the ever changing conditions with which Jews are confronted. Our position does not require a belief that in all or even most respects twentieth-century Jews know more or are more ethical than previous generations of Jews. To be sure, on some issues—the equality of the sexes, for example, or the abolition of slavery—we believe that our ethical values transcend those of our ancestors. Our historical perspective, however, cautions us against making such claims too often and too confidently—for we are the products of our times as our ancestors were the products of theirs.

Thus, we do not claim that we understand God better than Isaiah or that our sense of justice transcends that of Joseph Karo. Rather, we think that because our environment is different from our ancestors', we must transform their beliefs and practices into a contemporary idiom. When those beliefs and practices are transformed in this way, they can function for us as they did for earlier generations. Thus, Reconstructionists are involved in a sensitive balancing act, in which we seek to reinterpret the past in a contemporary form without discarding the treasury of wisdom embedded in Jewish civilization.

Once we recognize the evolution that Jewish civilization has undergone over three thousand years, we can begin to sense its power and resiliency. Jews have been able to live among so many different peoples with different cultures because of the ability of the Jewish people to take elements from the outside culture and adapt them for our purposes without losing our essential character.

One can illustrate this idea by looking at the holiday of Ḥanukah. Originally a commemoration of a historical event (probably a victory in a Jewish civil war), Ḥanukah took on different meanings in different eras. It attached itself to the time of the winter solstice where, like Christmas, it replaced a pagan festival which brought light to the dark winter. Its original significance was deemphasized by later tradition, which did not glorify human victory in war, and its celebration was commemorated by a special *haftarah* (prophetic reading) which states, "not by might, nor by power, but by my spirit, says the Lord of Hosts." In modern times, Ḥanukah was revived both by Zionists who wanted to glorify Jewish efforts in military endeavors, and by Jews integrated into Christian society, who needed a counterpart to Christmas.

Conscious Changes

All of our holidays, practices, and even beliefs have evolved, and they must continue to evolve if Judaism is to stay vital in today's world. While it has always been the case that Judaism has been adapted, this generally has been an unself-conscious process; Jews for much of our history believed that innovations actually were more accurate understandings of the original Torah. What has changed fundamentally is that we are now conscious of the changes. Today we must live and work with the awareness that we ourselves can and do make changes.

In essence, this is the challenge of the modern era. In many ways, that knowledge makes the inevitable changes more difficult, but not less inevitable. Kaplan recognized the nature of this radical difference brought about by modernity, and challenged us in turn to face it. When we accept the definition of Judaism as an evolving religious civilization, we begin to come to terms with the enormity of the task of renewing Judaism for our time. In a world that is changing ever more quickly, we too must change more quickly to keep up.

If we accept the fact that Judaism evolves—and that change is essential to Jewish life—we might be led to the extreme position that nothing in Judaism has remained constant, or that change is the only constant factor. This would be an erroneous assumption. From the Reconstructionist perspective, what is constant in Judaism is the Jewish people and its devotion to the highest ideals of its religious civilization. The Jewish people who share in this devotion should determine in any given era what Judaism will be like. Of course, we must continue to be deeply immersed in the worlds of our ancestors as well as in our own world; thus, Judaism at any given time becomes a blend of our inheritance, of our own experiences, and of our vision of the future.

This outlook presumes a tremendous amount of faith in the ability of the Jewish people to survive and sustain itself. It also places a great responsibility on the individual Jew to be part of this process of continuing Jewish survival. We do not believe that the survival of the Jewish people is an end in itself. When Kaplan defined Judaism as the religion of ethical nationhood, he sought to express our conviction that Jewish civilization is a means to greater ends—the fulfillment of the individual, the responsibility of individuals to treat others as reflections of the divine image, and the responsibility of each community to seek global justice and peace among all communities. To be true to our heritage, we need to do more than empha-size Jewish survival; we must also make the Jewish civilization function in the service of these transcendent and immutable ends. That is why the tradition cannot be left to speak in archaic, irrelevant idioms, and that is why we cannot shirk the responsibility to become part of the process of the evolution of the Jewish people.

Despite those around us who study rates of Jewish births and inter-marriage and make dire predictions, despite the troubled and perilous condition of Jews in the State of Israel and elsewhere, Reconstruc-tionists today maintain an optimistic view concerning the future sur-vival of the Jewish people. We believe that Kaplan's definition is fundamentally sound, as long as the Jewish people maintains its will to survive.

The question that remains to be addressed is how we, the Jewish people, should go about reconstructing a Judaism for our day that will make us want to perpetuate ourselves—that will make us feel that we are passing a good heritage to the next generation.

CHAPTER THREE

THE CONCEPT OF GOD

Although religion is paramount in the Reconstructionist definition of Jewish civilization, conspicuously absent from our definition of Judaism is any mention of God. This is no accident. Reconstructionists believe that it is the Jewish people that is the constant which runs through all the various stages in the evolution of Jewish civilization. Jewish conceptions of God have changed through the centuries over the course of our historical odyssey. Even the claim that God is One has acquired different meanings: the midrashic writer's *Shekhinah* (divine presence) weeping in exile, the medieval philosopher's unchanging One, and the kabbalist's *sefirot* (divine emanations) provide little basis for the claim of theological uniformity. To *define* Jews in terms of their beliefs about God is thus impossible, unless we choose to distort the reality of the Jewish experience.

Though precise definitions of God are not Jewish touchstones, it is nevertheless the case that Jewish people have always believed in God and that that belief has been central to living a meaningful Jewish life. Today, developing a concept of God for oneself is an important part of one's self-understanding as a Jew.

Kaplan's Belief

Mordecai Kaplan had a distinctive and controversial concept of God. Although not all Reconstructionists share Kaplan's theology, an understanding of it may be helpful in challenging us to discover what God means to each of us.

Kaplan himself was raised to be a believing Jew. In the world in which he lived, God's presence gave meaning to the Jew's life. God was perceived as Creator of the universe, Revealer of the Torah, and Arbiter of the destiny of the Jewish people. God commanded the Jew to behave in certain ways; without God's command, those rituals and behaviors would have been meaningless. God set the destiny of the Jewish people; without that role in the world, being Jewish would have been meaningless. In ways that are incomprehensible to many of us today, God's assistance was sought at every turn, and changes of fortune were attributed to God's will. One spent hours of one's day in prayerful conversation with God and in the study of texts believed to be of divine authorship. Truly, one could thereby perceive the whole world as divinely inhabited.

Yet as a young man, Kaplan began to doubt the efficacy of this traditional world view for his life. Like so many other people, he could not believe the literal truth of the claims of the Jewish tradition. He began to doubt, for example, that God literally spoke to human beings and that those words were recorded in our sacred texts. He could not believe that the destinies of human beings are determined by an Almighty Person who is conscious of and concerned with our every human thought and action. He became skeptical of the prospect that God rewards and punishes us both in this life and, after death, in the World to Come. Unwilling to accept the explanation that biblical language and anthropomorphism could be dealt with as metaphor alone, Kaplan sought other answers couched in the language and thinking of his day.

Influenced by religious naturalism, Kaplan began thinking of God less as a Person who controls the world from above, and more as a Force or Process within the universe. In one significant way, this perception of God was true to the Jewish tradition. As early as the rabbinic period, Jews began to interpret biblical descriptions metaphorically. Yet, denying God as a Person who directs the affairs of the world, and particularly who acts in relation to the Jewish people, was a radical departure from the main currents of the tradition.

Despite claims to the contrary, Kaplan never denied the existence of God. Rather, he rejected the belief that God is a Person—a Being with thoughts and feelings like those of humans, who is aware of and concerned with the everyday affairs of the world. He found this traditional supernaturalistic concept impossible to believe, and he sought to reconstruct the Jewish concept of God precisely so that educated, modern-minded Jews would *not* abandon their belief in God. He thus described God in categories that did not require him to forsake his intellect.

Functional Reinterpretation

To understand Kaplan's discussion of God, one needs to understand the method he used to reinterpret the tradition. He did not believe that a contemporary Jew is *absolutely* free to attribute new palatable meanings to traditional concepts and rituals. Rather, he argued that it is our task to understand and empathize with the components of the tradition, so that we can determine how beliefs functioned for our ancestors in their own terms. Once that is accomplished, authentic reinterpretation would express in our terms the functional equivalents of what Jews in the past had expressed in their own idioms. For example, if the retelling of the Exodus story at the Pesaḥ Seder served as a device to liberate Jews and to have them confront the meaning of freedom, then it is authentic for us today to discuss the meaning of freedom at the Seder.

In the case of God-belief, Kaplan asserted that traditional conceptions of God had served Jews in the past by guiding them to salvation. By salvation, we mean those things for which people ultimately search: to find holiness, meaning, and peace in life; to bring about the betterment of the world.

In the traditional conception, God's Torah guides the individual to the sought-after goals, in this world and the next. Through God's redemption of the people Israel, the world will become a better place.

In Kaplan's functional reinterpretation, God becomes "the Power that makes for Salvation." Kaplan located God in the powers that direct people in the search for salvation. He emphasized the ways that God should *function* in people's lives. His main goal was to foster Judaism as the vehicle through which Jewish people work to achieve the goal of salvation.

Transnaturalism

Kaplan believed that the divine works through nature and human beings. He neither identified God with things in the world (natural) nor did he consider God to be beyond or detached from the world (supernatural). Therefore, Kaplan's theology came to be called "transnatural."

In this view, there is more to the universe than the sum of its parts. In the organic interrelationship of all of its laws, there are divine powers which truly exist apart from the empirically verifiable phenomena of nature. They are manifest, for example, in human self-consciousness. It takes a faith in God to believe that the world is structured in a way that gives significance to the human quest for salvation. A transnaturalist, however, believes that God works *through* us rather than *upon* us. Thus, our sense of responsibility to bring divinity into the world is sustained by the sense that there is a power at the source of human endeavors.

In more recent years, one of Kaplan's students, Rabbi Harold Schulweis, has developed a new means of expressing transnaturalistic belief that he calls "predicate theology." In grammatical terms, he suggests that we refer to God not as subject, but as predicate. This linguistic change liberates us to think about God in new ways. Using Schulweis's terminology, we would say that it is more important, for example, to believe that justice, kindness, and compassion are godly, than that God is a Person possessing the attributes of justice, kindness, and compassion. This is another way of expressing the importance of human responsibility to bring *godliness* into the world. Similarly, we refer in our prayers to God as the Healer of the sick. We express our hope in this way that the divine forces that heal will be effective. We also affirm our commitment to making those forces manifest—both through modern medicine and through our will to live.

This type of belief is not all that different from the conception of God held by such medieval philosophers as Maimonides, who is recognized universally as one of the great authorities for all Jews. Maimonides developed a theory of negative attributes because he understood that God cannot be described as subject. He conceived of God as immaterial, unchanging, and unaware of the details of this world. He believed that our knowledge of God could be derived only from our understanding of the divine laws which inhere in the universe. The Reconstructionist conception of God is thus not as radically discontinuous with the past as might be expected at first.

A transnaturalistic faith also answers one of the most troubling questions human beings have ever asked: If God is the force behind everything and controls all events, why do the innocent suffer? Another of Kaplan's students, Rabbi Harold Kushner, has given a contemporary transnaturalist's response to this question in his popular work, *When Bad Things Happen to Good People*. The answer is that the question itself is based on a faulty assumption. God is neither all-powerful nor present everywhere. Rather, as the nineteenth-century Hasidic master Rabbi Menahem Mendel of Kotsk teaches, "God dwells where we let God in." God is only manifest in the world where and when we ourselves approach salvation. God is not a Person who rewards and punishes us like a parent.

The innocent may suffer because we have not worked hard enough to end the suffering of the earth's creatures, or because random things occur over which neither we nor God have any control. Some ills—like war and famine—are subject to our redeeming efforts. Others—like death and natural disasters—can be ameliorated at best. When we can assist those in need or prevent needless pain,

God is working through us. When we cannot, it may be said that God weeps with us.

Questioning Transnaturalism

Some may wonder if transnaturalists aren't just pretending—that they don't really believe that God exists and only choose to call human activities "godly." After so many centuries in which God was conceived supernaturally, it does sometimes seem that a God without supernaturalism is no God at all. What good is God if God neither intervenes in human history to reward, punish, and effect His purposes, nor abides in a celestial realm, listening attentively to prayers? If God does not perform miracles, why pray for recovery when you are sick? If God does not command us, why should we perform ritual acts at all? Actually, transnaturalists have good reasons to retain a faith in God, to perform rituals, and to pray.

It does require an act of faith to be a Reconstructionist. No one can demonstrate scientifically or prove rationally that there are divine powers that make for salvation. When a tyrant is deposed, when a poet composes a verse, when a human relationship flourishes, when a person achieves a liberating insight—all these phenomena could be explained merely in terms of natural causes and effects. Belief in the existence of a transnatural God, however, enables us to derive strength because we view such occurrences in a larger context. They are the accomplishment of divine ends—bringing love, justice, and beauty into the world. Only a person who devotes a great deal of *kavvanah* (intention) and energy to living in harmony with the divine laws of the universe can know from experience how very real God is, conceived transnaturally.

Critics of transnaturalism have suggested that this approach to God is cold and impersonal; that in explaining God in this manner, God is reduced to a concept; and that this process undermines the awe and mystery present in the traditional Jewish view of God. But what could be more awe-inspiring than the feeling one gets when one senses oneself being the conduit of a power working in the universe to make it a better place to live? Or when one perceives the power working through nature which enables the trees to grow or flowers to bloom? And what could be more mysterious than the way in which those processes unfold themselves? Transnaturalism doesn't reduce God to a concept; it provides human beings with a language with which to speak of God as at work within the world, rather than hovering over it. It allows human beings truly to see themselves as partners in creation.

Uncommanded Mitzvot

Transnaturalism rejects the belief that the words of the Torah come from divine revelation at Sinai or that the *mitzvot* are each divinely ordained commandments. From a transnaturalist viewpoint, God is not an omnipotent commander who rewards and punishes. What then is the rationale for obeying Jewish laws? What does it mean, for example, to address God as the one who commands us to light Shabbat candles? In what sense are we commanded?

The answer to this question is found in our initial definition of what it means to see oneself as part of the Jewish people. We behave as Jews because we value our connections to Jewish people, past and present. Jewish rituals have a sacred history that reflect inherited wisdom as well as group renewal. They should not be discarded casually. Otherwise, each generation could begin anew rather than reconstruct.

We often choose to retain the traditional forms of Jewish practice, even when we no longer mean what our ancestors meant when they spoke those words or performed those actions. We do so because such rituals both enrich us and sustain us—leading to our salvation in terms of our own values. Sanctified by the intentionality of our ancestors, the ritual forms themselves are permeated with a sacred aura that is ideally suited to help us deepen our connections to the divine presence.

Thus, when we light the Shabbat candles, we do more than symbolize the beginning of a day of rest devoted to our ultimate values. The flickering candles themselves possess a power to transform us because of the *kavvanot* (meanings) that past generations attributed to those candles: for example, the identification of that light with the *Shekhinah* (divine presence) or the experience of receiving a *neshamah yeterah*—an additional soul that enables the Jew to reach greater spiritual heights on Shabbat.

Meanings beget new meanings. The sense of being commanded comes to us through traditional forms that give us a clearer vision of the divine imperatives in our own era. For example, the Shabbat candles remind us that fire is both life-giving and destructive, and that the messianic hope of the Shabbat depends on our ability to harness our technology for constructive purposes. If God is not the commander of these acts, God nonetheless is reflected through them.

Prayer

If God does not hear and answer prayer, how and why do Reconstructionists worship?

This question, often asked, is based on a mistaken assumption. It is not the case that the primary purpose of prayer in Judaism is to petition God to grant one's pleas. The Hebrew verb "to pray" (*lehitpallel*) is in a grammatically reflexive form which usually indicates an action which one performs by and for oneself. Accordingly, most rationales given for prayer throughout Jewish history have asserted that praying improves the moral and spiritual character of the one who prays.

Thus a Reconstructionist is acting traditionally when s/he expresses gratitude, humility, or wonder in prayer, even as the words of the liturgy are seen as metaphors which evoke the highest aspirations of the Jewish people. A goal of prayer is to develop those qualities by tapping into the divine power that enables us to become more appreciative, humble, etc. Prayer always has functioned to make us aware of the divine presence, and so it continues to function. We seek to unite ourselves with the transnatural One that exists and works within us.

Moreover, communal worship services have an additional function for Reconstructionists, who are most interested in building a sense of Jewish community. The words and melodies of the liturgy allow us both to express our common aspirations, hopes, and frustrations, and to share in an aesthetically satisfying Jewish activity. When we use the words of past generations to express our contemporary concerns, we develop an empathy with the insights and concerns of our ancestors, as well as a bond with all Jews living today.

Myth and Metaphor

Many Reconstructionists have difficulty accepting Kaplan's approach to God in all of its facets, and it is not necessary to do so to identify with the Reconstructionist movement. Reconstructionist congregations—and the Reconstructionist Rabbinical College— include many spiritually-oriented Jews who find Kaplan's identification of God as *Process* alienating. When they *davven* at worship services, and when they attempt to pursue lives of sanctification, they experience God as a *Person* with whom they can, in some sense, converse, and from whom they can derive strength and fortitude. That understanding can fit into Reconstructionist thought as long as it does not include affirmation of Torah-from-Sinai and direct supernatural intervention in our individual lives.

Though there is much debate among Reconstructionists about the language and imagery of prayer, the debate is *not* about supernaturalism. It is rather about the way prayer can and should function to express mythically what is beyond exact description.

All Reconstructionists would agree, for example, that though we refer to God as the Healer of the sick, we should not accept our ancestors' conception of God as supernaturally intervening to perform miraculous cures. Yet after the physician has administered the prescribed treatment, there is an unpredictable variable, so that not all patients respond identically. The energy of the struggle for life rises and subsides in ways that cannot be measured. Kaplan would have described that struggle in terms of impersonal life forces; other Reconstructionists choose to describe it in terms of a personal God who transcends nature. Both would agree that God does not consciously and intentionally intervene to suspend the laws of nature in order to reward and punish. The debate, then, is *not* about supernatural intervention. It is, rather, about whether God, who is beyond accurate description, should be described metaphorically as Person.

Kaplan and earlier generations of his disciples cared most of all about intellectual integrity, and they fought the battle on the issue of the words of our prayers: We should not, they argued, ever say what we do not mean. A new generation shares that commitment but is often more inclined to use traditional formulations because of their mythic and poetic power to move us—even though we don't understand those phrases in terms of the supernatural idiom of our ancestors. The laws of nature, after all, include not only those phenomena which scientists can measure, but also the laws of the human psyche. It is therefore possible for a modern-minded naturalistic Jew to affirm the value and centrality of mystical consciousness, and the related therapeutic importance of prayerful intentionality.

Chosenness and Vocation

Not all of Jewish doctrine about God is so easily assimilated to a Reconstructionist world view. If we cannot say that God chose the Jewish people, why do we consider ourselves chosen? How can we bless God for having "separated us from all other peoples of the earth, and not cast our lot with theirs?"

Kaplan's response was that we should not do so, and the prayerbooks of the Reconstructionist movement do not include references to the chosenness of Israel. This meant changing the words of some of the most central and best loved prayers: the Kiddush (the sanctification over wine) recited on Shabbat and holiday evenings, the blessing said when called to the Torah, the Havdalah prayer recited at the close of Shabbat, and the *Alenu* prayer, with which every worship service is brought to a close.

In place of chosenness, the editors of the Reconstructionist prayerbooks substituted the concept of vocation. Instead of regarding the Jews as "chosen from among all peoples," we understand ourselves —and all peoples—as being "called to do God's work." That is to say, we follow a specific path to salvation through the preservation and development of our inherited tradition. Other peoples follow their own paths; ours is not necessarily superior to theirs, nor can we be certain that, on any particular issue, it is divinely grounded.

In this context, the traditional belief that there is a *brit*, a covenant, between God and Israel, is usefully revalued. Reconstructionists do not accept literally that the Torah includes the unchanging and everlasting terms of the Jewish people's responsibilities to God. We can speak, however, of an evolving Jewish understanding of covenant—a holy relationship grounded in mutual trust and respect, modeled on the biblical relationship between God and Israel—and about the responsibilities of Jews to behave, ethically and ritually, as if they were covenanted to do so. We can also speak of a multicovenant theology, through which we recognize that other peoples have developed their own distinctive covenantal approaches to human responsibility.

As with other liturgical changes, Reconstructionists continue to debate whether these particular emendations are necessary. The debate should not, however, be misunderstood. The question is *not* whether Reconstructionists should return to a claim of superiority for the Jewish tradition. It is rather about mythic and metaphorical language in the liturgy and whether it is possible to reinterpret without changing the words.

Why did chosenness require special attention when so much else in the prayerbook was left alone, to be understood metaphorically? The motivation for these liturgical changes was ethical. Kaplan and his disciples were concerned that a sense of chosenness might degenerate too easily into chauvinism, self-righteousness, and unfounded claims of ethnic superiority. They believed that the ultimate salvation of the Jewish people is interdependent with the salvation of all peoples, and they thus were concerned that Jews not insulate themselves from their neighbors.

Clearly, the Jewish belief that we are the chosen people has been central to the identities of countless generations of Jews. We have believed that the Torah is a gift from God, and that God chose us from among all the peoples because we were willing to enter into a covenant, agreeing to live according to the divine commandments. Thus, the notion of chosenness has functioned in the past to validate and give meaning to the Jewish way of life. To be sure, we were never supposed to believe that *Jews* were *superior;* only that our Torah is the true and only complete reflection of the divine will. Later, when Jews were subjected to persecution and to Christian missionizing in the rabbinic and medieval periods, the belief in the exclusive value of the Torah gave our ancestors the strength to resist apostasy and despair.

Given the circumstances of liberal North American Jews—who neither wish to live separately from their non-Jewish neighbors, nor believe that *any* religious tradition is divinely revealed in a literal sense—our task is to discover the functional equivalent of the Chosen People doctrine. How can we express the unique value of Judaism so that Jews will be moved to greater Jewish commitment, without simultaneously implying that one religion is inherently better than another? Clearly, the Reconstructionist does not want to resort to God the Chooser for validation; all persons and peoples manifest the divine when they actualize their "salvation," and the expression of their insights and images is conditioned by their respective civilizations. But if Judaism is not superior, some will ask, then why should a Jew remain Jewish?

Reconstructionists answer this question, first, by referring to the richness of the Jewish tradition. So many Jews are virtually ignorant of the depths of Jewish spirituality, the beauty of Jewish poetry, the sensibility of Jewish ethics and law, the pathos of the Jewish experience. When a Jewish person comes to know and live the tradition and thereby enriches his/her life, this is the basis for a far more important and authentic claim than one based on ignorant retention of a sense of superiority.

Jews live Jewish lives because they want to feel at home in the tradition, to see and experience the world with the insights of the Jewish outlook. Some also want to claim that their way is better than all others, but Reconstructionists think such a claim borders on immaturity. It is possible for a healthy individual to retain a good self-image without simultaneously denigrating the worth of others. Similarly, it is better for Jews to retain a healthy respect for other traditions—and to interact with them and their adherents—even as they take pride and derive meaning from their own tradition. It is possible and desirable to be "centered" without claiming to be the center of the universe. Only when all peoples learn this lesson will we achieve the equivalent of the messianic era.

CHAPTER FOUR

THE PAST HAS A VOTE, NOT A VETO

Kaplan's views on chosenness stand out in contrast to his attempts to reconstruct most other elements of Jewish life. It was a rare instance in which he felt strongly that a concept was not amenable to reconstruction and had to be altered radically. For the most part, radical alteration was not the desirable reconstruction that Kaplan sought or envisioned. In fact, Kaplan personally remained a traditionally observant Jew throughout his lifetime.

The criterion by which Jewish life was to be reconstructed can be described by Kaplan's epigram, "The past has a vote, not a veto." Understanding what Kaplan meant by that phrase is the first step in developing the model for the reconstruction of Jewish life which must be pursued in every generation.

The Authority of the Past

"The past has a vote, not a veto." That is the answer to the question: What is the authority of the past? Preceding generations attributed the authority of the tradition to divine revelation. The Written and Oral Torah were seen as the record of God's will as it was revealed to Moses and Israel at Mount Sinai. Thus, the very notion of innovation was discouraged. All ancient and medieval innovators claimed —and believed—that they were but recovering and restoring the original meaning of the Sinaitic revelation. As the Jewish people adapted to new, changing circumstances and Jewish civilization evolved, our ancestors engaged in what Kaplan called "transvaluation"—claiming ancient authority for new insights.

Today, our awareness of historical forces makes us, in this respect, radically discontinuous with the ahistorical consciousness of our ancestors. To claim that Judaism is an evolving civilization is to acknowledge that people and traditions change in response to historical circumstances. When we innovate today, we do so consciously and with the awareness that we ourselves are shaped by our milieu just as our ancestors were shaped by theirs. We engage in conscious "revaluation," in Kaplan's terms, rather than in our ancestors' "transvaluation."

But Reconstructionists are not dispassionate historians who claim objectivity. While we attempt to understand the experience at Sinai, for example, by striving to recover the social, political, cultural, and psychological forces that shaped Moses and the Israelites, we do not claim that the divine voice they heard was the projection of their primitive imagination. We acknowledge the existence of God and thus the reality of divine-human encounter. What we deny is that the records of such revelatory encounters are transcripts of God's speech. God, it will be recalled, is discovered quite naturally by humans who seek God. Thus, the content of a revelation is the record of a particular human quest and discovery; the evolution of Jewish civilization is the natural progression of successive generations of Jewish people who have sought and found God in their own terms.

Seen in this light, the value of the past is considerable. The Jewish tradition is a record of the insights of prophets and sages through the generations. Neither human nature nor the nature of the divine has changed over the millenia; only the concepts and idioms through which Jews understand the world have evolved. Thus, we strive to translate the insights we have inherited from the Jewish past into our own terms and thereby to revalue inherited beliefs and practices, so that we can enrich our lives through them. Reconstructionists who observe the Shabbat and holiday cycle of the Jewish year, for example, do so in order to immerse themselves in the sacred forms and calendrical rhythms with which our ancestors shaped their world. There is more to the Jewish outlook than a series of propositions to be judged true or false. Judaism is a civilization which communicates and acculturates on a host of nonverbal levels.

When Past and Present Conflict

The process of revaluation is no simple task. For all the brilliance and depth of insight of our ancestors, their values are often not applicable in a straightforward way. They are occasionally even repugnant from our perspective. Kaplan insisted that we preserve and observe Jewish customs and values as long as they continue to serve as a vehicle towards salvation—the enhancement of the meaning and purposefulness of our existence.

When a particular Jewish value or custom is found wanting in this respect, it is our obligation as Jews to find a means to reconstruct it—to adopt innovative practices or find new meanings in old ones.

That the past has a vote means that we must struggle to hear the voices of our ancestors. What did this custom or that idea mean to them? How did they see the presence of God in it? How can we retain or regain its importance in our own lives? That the past does not have a veto means that we must struggle to hear our own voices as distinct from theirs. What might this custom or that idea mean to us today? As participants in a secular civilization, how can we incorporate our values into our lives as Jews?

It is clear that our ties to our Jewish past and our sense of the secular present often pull us in opposite directions. Reconstructionists seek to find ways to merge those two sensibilities while remaining true to both of them. Kaplan's statement that the past does not have a veto implies that tradition is susceptible to adaptation. Innovation need not entail the destruction of tradition; on the contrary, change is an important part of keeping tradition alive, as it has been throughout Jewish history. As the world changes faster, Judaism must be reconstructed ever more quickly if its wisdom is to continue to guide us.

Post-halakhic Judaism

By contemporary definitions, one cannot define Reconstructionism as a halakhic form of Judaism. If halakhah were defined as the Jewish process of transmitting tradition, then we certainly could see ourselves within the framework of halakhah. Unfortunately, today the term has taken on the meaning of a rigid body of law, changeable only under rarefied circumstances. In past generations and other eras of Jewish life, halakhah functioned as we think it should today: though in theory it was seen as immutable law, in fact it served as a body of tradition which could adapt to the needs of the Jewish people throughout the ages.

We also question the effectiveness of the halakhic method itself for dealing with contemporary concerns. The halakhic method presumes that all questions are answerable with reference to legal precedent. It ignores the possibility that new issues, while they may be guided by old values, must be discussed with reference to the world in which we now live.

Furthermore, Jewish teachings no longer function for us as law, nor can they be expected to do so. For law to function, it must have a body of people to create and adjudicate it; there must be sanctions if one disobeys. Nowhere in the world does Jewish law now function in that way. In tightly-woven Orthodox communities, the members choose *voluntarily* to place themselves "under the yoke of the law," and can choose to leave at any time. Even in Israel, where Jewish law functions for issues of personal status, the law can be circumvented. Therefore, thinking of halakhah as binding law is misleading in today's world.

Finally, this change in social circumstances is not accidental. It reflects a basic value of Western democracy—that individuals ought to make religious choices autonomously. Our ancestors believed that the ideal Jew was one who subordinated his/her own independent judgment and instead behaved in accordance with the will of God. By contrast, we believe that moral and spiritual faculties are actualized best when the individual makes his/her own choices. Thus, even if there were an opportunity to return to an authoritarian community in which the traditional *mitzvot* were enforced coercively, we would not choose to do so.

To be true to ourselves we must understand the differences in perception between us and those who have gone before, while retaining a reverence for the tradition they fashioned. If we can juxtapose those things, we ensure that the past will have a vote, but not a veto. It is important to describe some examples of how this principle is to operate in practical terms. How might a Reconstructionist adopt an approach to a matter of ritual or ethical difficulty?

At the outset, it should be made clear that we must speak about a particular person with a Reconstructionist outlook, and *not* the Reconstructionist position on a given issue. Although the Reconstructionist movement strongly advocates that Reconstructionist groups consider these questions together, Reconstructionism ultimately is an *approach* to Judaism. We learn and appreciate what the tradition has to say, we come to a spectrum of options that reflects that understanding, and the organizations of the movement may even issue a set of guidelines. But ultimately we believe that in all cases, be they questions of ritual or principle, individuals must decide for themselves about the proper Jewish way to proceed in a given situation. While we may share certain values and certain life situations, no two sets of circumstances are identical. We hope that the Reconstructionist process works to help people find the right answers for themselves; but we can only assist in helping individuals to ask the right questions so that their choices are made in an informed way within a Jewish context.

Ethical Dilemmas

What then would be the process of ethical decision making? To begin with, we would examine our own intellectual, emotional, and moral preconceptions, so that we can be honest about our own viewpoints. Otherwise, we will be forever trying to force the tradition to agree with us, or looking only for ways in which it does. This is unconscious transvaluation—looking to the past for justification of the way we wish to behave—rather than the desired conscious revaluation.

Second, we would do a thorough search of Jewish law to ascertain whether or not there is a halakhic position on the issue, how it was derived, and upon what Jewish values it was based. Obviously, this part demands a great deal of knowledge about the sources and how to use them.

We then would compare those two conclusions. If they are consonant, we might want to stop the process there. If they are dissonant, we probably would examine things further. We might ask ourselves on what values we base our intuitive responses. Are they Jewish values? Are there Jewish values which suggest a different conclusion from that derived from the halakhic process? This last set of questions is at the core of revaluation.

Abortion

As an example, let us look at the issues raised by abortion. Jane Cohen, who is pregnant with her second child, undergoes amniocentesis and discovers that she is carrying a Tay-Sachs child. Both she and her husband Robert wish her to have an abortion. They don't want this unborn child to suffer a wrongful life and a painful death.

The Cohens bring their crisis to a support group within their Reconstructionist congregation. With the assistance of a rabbinic resource person, the group studies the halakhic position: this is not grounds for an abortion. Based on the argument of the sanctity of life, no life may be considered wrongful. Abortion of a potential life cannot be sanctioned under these circumstances. The only universally recognized halakhic warrant for abortion is if the mother's life itself is in danger.

The couple is deeply distraught. Not only must they consider doing something very difficult, but they must do so knowing it contravenes halakhah. Then the group begins the process of revaluation. Are there other possibilities within the Jewish value system which might provide a different outlook?

First, they consider the value of *shelom bayit*, concord in the household. What does it mean in this situation? Would it be possible for the Cohens to live with the tension created by the birth of this child? What would the effects be on their marriage? On the sibling? What kind of financial and emotional strains would occur? There is precedent in Jewish tradition for permitting abortion when the health of the mother, mental or physical, is seriously in question. There is also precedent for abortion when a nursing sibling would be deprived of adequate nourishment because of the pregnancy. The principle of *shelom bayit* might be extended to cover these and other possibilities, such as the feelings of the father and his ability to handle the situation, or the marriage itself to tolerate the stress.

Second, there is the concept of *tzelem Elohim*, that we are created in God's image. Sanctity of life must be balanced with quality of life. It is necessary at least to consider the possibility that giving birth to a child who will suffer pain and die an early death might not be promoting the sanctity of life created in God's image. This is certainly a more difficult possibility to entertain from a Jewish perspective, and must be done with great caution.

An exploration of this case would lead the Cohens to consider the ramifications of their actions and to understand them in terms of a larger value system. It would provide them with the kind of communal support necessary to make a decision such as this. It would also grant them the dignity of knowing that the decision is theirs to make, and that they would receive communal support regardless of what they decided.

The group might even want to take the process a step further, helping the Cohens to find a meaningful ritual to support them in their decision—a ceremony after the abortion, or a special welcoming ceremony, if they decided to go through with the difficult birth. These are some of the possibilities opened up by the process of revaluation.

Ritual Decisions

Does this process work for ritual decisions as well? What about the case of Miriam Feinberg, who is getting more involved in Jewish life but for whom *kashrut* (Jewish dietary observance) is difficult? She would begin by examining all the feelings she has about *kashrut*. Let us assume Miriam sees no value in *kashrut*. She can't imagine why one would go to the expense of buying kosher meat or two sets of dishes; she can't figure out why certain products aren't kosher; she has no desire to give up eating or cooking some of her favorite foods.

The Reconstructionist approach would suggest that Miriam familiarize herself with the halakhah about *kashrut*—preferably with a group of people in a Reconstructionist context who are struggling with the same issue.

Since her own intuition and the tradition obviously are in conflict, a process of revaluation is in order. That revaluation, in case of a ritual practice, has two components—one intellectual and the other experiential. First, the group would want to seek out new meanings for the observance of *kashrut*. A list might include: making one's home more Jewish, allowing anyone to eat in one's home, getting in touch with Jewish tradition, making eating something one does with more attention, becoming aware of *tza'ar ba'alei hayyim*—the traditional concern with the pain of living creatures, supporting the kosher food industry so that Jews who choose to keep kosher can do so. They would then want to experiment with keeping kosher, perhaps with meals they cooked together or eating out in a restaurant and ordering only "kosher" items, or learning how to make their dishes and utensils kosher, or buying a kosher cookbook and making special meals.

Eventually, they might choose to keep some portion of the traditions of *kashrut*, as opposed to attempting to take on all of them. They might, for example, eat only kosher foods but not have special dishes, keep kosher only in the home, choose specific foods from which to refrain, or buy only kosher meat.

In addition, the group might decide that, apart from variations in personal observance of *kashrut*, the synagogue ought to serve as a repository for more traditional practice, and that *kashrut* should be observed in the communal kitchen. But how then can members with non-kosher homes be included in communal celebrations? The process for making such collective decisions is discussed in Chapter Ten.

The group might also be led to a more radical conclusion. Perhaps after all the discussion and experimentation, they are left with the sense that keeping kosher is not for them. Though they do not want their Judaism to permeate their lives in this way, they nevertheless want to make some Jewish value statement about eating. This might lead the group to develop a new system of manners and mores regarding food that would be their *kashrut*—their way of sanctifying and bringing meaning to their lives. Would this still be Jewish?

As Reconstructionists, we can't answer definitively or with finality. With any new practice, only time and experience will tell. If their *kashrut* became standard practice for many Jews, that would be the case. If it did not, it would mean that it was not a good way of expressing Jewishness through eating.

What we as Reconstructionists must assert is that we do not fear such innovation. It is healthy for the Jewish people to revaluate: to look for meanings beneath the surface of extant rituals; to look for new rituals which better express old meanings. This process will keep Judaism a vibrant and living tradition within which there are and will continue to be many forms of self-expression.

CHAPTER FIVE

LIVING IN TWO CIVILIZATIONS

The basis for reconstructing the traditional Jewish concepts of God, Torah, and Israel is the series of insights that grew out of the political emancipation of contemporary Jews, our exposure to Western intellectual disciplines, and our social integration as responsible citizens of the Western democracies. In this chapter, we shall present the Reconstructionist view of democracy and of the appropriate attitudes that Jews might take towards the larger, secular society.

The Open Society

Many people have postulated that Judaism can only survive in a hostile environment—that anti-Semitism is the main reason that Jews have remained Jewish in the modern era. If only the democracies of Western Europe and North America had lived up to the original promise of emancipation, they claim, then it would have been only a matter of time before all Jews would have yielded to the enticements of assimilation. They point, on the one hand, to the hopes of assimilated Western European Jews before the rise of Nazism, and to the progressive assimilation of American Jews; and, on the other hand, to the renaissance of Jewish identification after the Holocaust and again after the 1967 Six Day War. They regard the openness of democratic societies as a threat to Jewish survival, and consciously or unconsciously, their program for Jewish survival depends upon convincing Jews to retain a certain degree of distrust for and alienation from non-Jewish culture and people. This sort of outlook, in its extreme form, becomes the basis for the embattled mentality of many contemporary Jews, who bemoan the progressive integration of Jews into North American society even as they support the attempts of Jewish organizations to eliminate the very discrimination against Jews that, according to this view, prevents their full integration.

Reconstructionists disagree with this negative understanding of the place of Jews in secular society. We believe that Judaism can survive and prosper in an environment that is supportive of or indifferent to Jewish interests. We are not unaware of the problems caused when Jews live in an open society. We believe, however, that it is self-deceptive and self-defeating for North American Jews to regard that open environment as hostile even as most Jews enjoy unprecedented prosperity. After all, most of us do not contemplate abandoning our current comfort to move to Israel, nor are we anxious to retreat into a segregated Jewish community. Moreover, as increasing numbers of Jews raised in assimilated homes seek ways to increase and intensify their Jewish identification, we believe that it is indeed possible for the Jewish community to flourish even in an open environment that offers Jews other options. We need not rely on anti-Semites; we can instead affect our own fate by reconstructing Judaism into a form that Jews will choose to embrace.

The Promise of America

Long before American Jews had successfully ascended the social, economic, educational, and political rungs of their society, Mordecai Kaplan recognized the promise of North American democracy for Jews. As the great immigration of Eastern European Jews was ending in the 1920s and American Jews were struggling for acceptance in the 1930s and 1940s, Kaplan declared that such democratic values as freedom, tolerance, equality, universal enfranchisement, and individual opportunity represented the most elevated form of political life yet developed by a society. While others, then as now, regarded the successful integration of Jews into democratic society as a mixed blessing—bewailing the loss of Yiddish, the rebellion against traditional practice, the replacement of Jewish learning by secular study —Kaplan saw an opportunity to integrate democratic values into a reconstructed Jewish civilization.

He called his program "living in two civilizations." Whereas in the past Jews had lived in segregated, autonomous Jewish communities and thus had been able to live completely in a single Jewish civilization, there was no denying that Jews who now found themselves in democratic societies lived primarily in a secular civilization— governed by American legislatures and courts, speaking English, singing American songs, working in secular environments with non-Jews, being educated in American schools, structuring their lives according to American values. Had we *also* been *required* to abandon our Jewish identities then we would have faced a critical threat to Jewish survival. In fact, however, the most wonderful aspect of democratic America is its pluralism—church and state are separate, white Anglo-Saxon founders accepted (at times reluctantly) waves of immigration by diverse ethnic, racial, and religious groups, and the Constitution protects their right to be different. This is, as Kaplan foresaw, truly a fertile environment in which Judaism can flourish in a new, democratic way.

For this new kind of civilization to thrive, however, Jews have to learn how to live in two civilizations. They live, of necessity, primarily in an American civilization. But because of the separation between church and state and because of America's tolerance of diverse cultural expression, they can also live in a Jewish civilization—worshipping and studying together, forming Jewish political and social organizations, providing Jewish social services, developing an American Jewish way of life parallel to the distinctive ways of life of other hyphenated Americans. Rejecting the melting pot metaphor long before it fell out of fashion, Kaplan argued that American civilization is attenuated; it cannot fill all of the needs of its citizens precisely because it has no established religion and expects its citizens to develop their own means of religious and ethnic expression. Its genius is that it is an umbrella civilization—structured to unify its diverse elements without forcibly homogenizing them.

Thus, Kaplan called upon Jews to embrace the open society—not only because its structural pluralism does not require the abandonment of Judaism, but also because American ideals at their best coincide with Jewish ideals as they ought to be developed and reconstructed. Jews have much to learn from America. Traditional Judaism contained elements of democratic values, but those elements were only imperfectly formed. For example, Jewish law respects the rights of the individual; medieval Jewish communities developed a variety of modes of representative government; traditional Jewish authority had not been centralized for a millenium, so that the customs and legal interpretations of one segment of Jewry were respected by other segments that followed different customs and interpretations.

Kaplan boldly sought to develop these democratic aspects of pre-modern Judaism into a full-blown democratic Jewish civilization. Halakhic authority, which had ceased to function, would be reconstructed through involving *all* Jews. He envisioned an organic Jewish *kehillah* that Jews would choose freely to join. Moreover, he believed it is in the best interest of Jews to contribute to a pluralistic America in which all groups unite in common civic values such as equality, tolerance, freedom, and pluralism.

Being Jewish and American

Thus in the Reconstructionist framework, it is not necessary to choose between one's Jewish and American identities. One can— indeed, one must—live in two civilizations. When the two civilizations are in harmony, this is both simple and effective. Just as we find meaning and value in celebrating Sukkot as Jews, so too we can find meaning and value in celebrating Thanksgiving as Americans. Both of these holidays have a similar meaning and purpose (giving thanks for abundance, reminding us of our obligation to care for those less fortunate) and have certain parallel observances (centered around the family meal in the sukkah or in the home). It might be argued that there is little need for celebrating both. Why bother to express oneself in two different idioms?

Living in two civilizations means seeing this redundancy as an advantage. One experience can illuminate the other. Seeing the similarities reminds us of the comfort of living as both Jews and Americans. It enables us to remain in contact with the world outside as well as with our deeply meaningful past. It gives us a language to share our celebration of Judaism with those who are not Jewish, and it can highlight the relevance of the Jewish celebration for this world. Furthermore, Thanksgiving and Sukkot remind us of our history and its lessons. We celebrate values developed by our ancestors—American and Jewish—out of their separate experiences, while affirming our attachment to both.

It is also the case that there are elements in each civilization that are not paralleled in the other. The Jewish civilization, for example, has placed little emphasis on athletics. Yet sports can provide catharsis, stimulation, and greater mental and physical health to participants and observers alike. Similarly, the American civilization has little to offer in terms of the life-cycle rituals—weddings, funerals, births, or even divorces—that are necessary to bring meaning to crucial events in life.

Furthermore, an American Jew can be heir to a Jewish tradition that yields insights into the divine aspects of the universe, provides enlightening struggles with complex ethical dilemmas, and gives a multifaceted system of ritual and devotional practice that can sanctify one's life and make connections between people. In its depth and richness, the Jewish tradition offers models of behavior and realms of discourse that are not available in contemporary secular culture. On the other hand, North American culture has much to offer—not only in terms of material prosperity and professional opportunity, but also in its literature, art, and cinema, in its respect for individual autonomy and liberty, and in its cosmopolitan amalgamation of diverse cultures.

More challenging are the situations in which living in two civilizations brings about conflict. Committed Jews in North America are faced with choices at every turn. Little league games conflict with religious school classes, golf tournaments with Shabbat services, and opera performances with Jewish lecture series. Parents must choose between paying Jewish day school tuition or saving for college tuition. With a limited amount of time and energy, membership on the Jewish community center board and participation in a political campaign may be mutually exclusive commitments.

Reconstructionists tend to welcome these choices as evidence of the rich opportunities available to us in North America. We do not seek to retreat into a parochial world, nor do we think that Jews ought to feel guilty for their desire to be full participants in the secular culture. Rather, we believe that Jewish civilization offers Jews a different kind of social, cultural, and spiritual enrichment that is not available elsewhere. When attending a Jewish lecture or concert offers that enrichment, Jews will choose to participate. They will do so not out of guilt or nostalgia, but out of excitement and satisfaction.

Education

The question of education in the context of two civilizations also creates a conflict. The first generation of Reconstructionists opposed the establishment of Jewish day schools in their belief that Jews should be in the vanguard of the continuing struggle to keep America true to its democratic, pluralistic ideals. All American children, they thought, should be educated together in the American civic values they share. Jewish identity could be nurtured adequately in supplementary afternoon and weekend schools, and primarily in the acculturating experiences of the Jewish home and community.

With hindsight, we now can see that this hope has not been realized. The progressive Americanization of Jews has made it unrealistic to rely exclusively upon Jewish families in which parents are often in need of Jewish education themselves. Nor can we depend upon supplementary religious schools faced with children tired after a day at school and resentful of time taken away from competing extracurricular activities.

The Reconstructionist response has been multifaceted. We have emphasized family programming such as the *shabbaton* (Sabbath retreat) and the Shabbat seder (a Friday night meal and ritual including the whole family). We have also long advocated summer camping. These programs expose young Jews to an authentic, all-embracing Jewish experience that they can then replicate on their own. The programs also involve parents, who can then learn together with their children. We have developed the ḥavurah—a small group of people who celebrate, study, worship, learn, and take on social justice projects together—as a way of recreating in a contemporary setting the warmth and activities of the traditional community. We have affirmed the importance of continuing adult education in the recognition that training that ends with bar/bat mitzvah or even confirmation leaves Jews with the impression that Judaism is only for children or adolescents.

Judaizing one's life is an ongoing process. Our educators have been at the forefront of educational innovations, adapting curricular and pedagogic models from the general culture to the needs of the Jewish school. And in 1973, the Federation of Reconstructionist Congregations and Havurot, reversing the movement's prior position, passed a resolution in support of the establishment of liberal Jewish day schools.

Day schools alone, however, will not be able to accomplish our goal of living in two civilizations. Minimally, they will have to avoid inculcating in their students a sense that Jews are and ought to be separate from their non-Jewish neighbors. Logically, that attitude eventuates either in *aliyah* (when Jews decide that Israel provides the only complete Jewish environment), or more frequently, in Jews who pursue their educations and professions in American society but who feel, in their heart of hearts, that their successful integration is a betrayal of their Jewish identity—what sociologist Charles Liebman has called "the ambivalent American Jew." Reconstructionists have articulated a unique vision of a day school that has yet to be implemented: a school in which American children from a variety of religious and ethnic groups would study together for half the day and then separate for the other half while they studied their own distinctive heritage, language, and history. Such a model would be grounded on the ideal that unity in diversity is the most exalted ethical course.

Social Action

Because of our embrace of the open society, Reconstructionists have viewed involvement in American social and political issues as integral to a vibrant and meaningful American Judaism. Just as we seek to democratize the Jewish community, so also do we recognize the need to bring the insights of the Jewish tradition to bear upon the issues that American society confronts.

It is well known that Jews in America have always been social activists—active in the labor and socialist movements a half-century ago, and more recently in the civil rights movement, the Vietnam peace movement, and the feminist movement. While there has been an observable trend more recently among Jews away from liberal causes and towards a more exclusive concern with Jewish and Israeli interests, our behavior in recent elections still shows that we do not vote primarily our pocketbooks—that we continue to display an extraordinary degree of concern for social, economic, and racial justice.

As Reconstructionists, we are concerned with building upon this phenomenon. It is not enough for American Jews to be socially concerned. If we are to pursue integrated lives in two civilizations, we should bring the values of the Jewish tradition to our social concerns. The Jewish values of *tzedakah* and *gemilut hasadim*, for example, are not identical to Christian charity or social democratic welfare. Our tradition's approach to the rights and responsibilities of individuals and societies is a largely untapped source of insights into contemporary questions about the social allocation of resources. These are visible in the resolutions of the Federation of Reconstructionist Congregations and Havurot, as well as in the editorials and articles in the *Reconstructionist* magazine. Similarly, the Shalom Center, an interdenominational Jewish center devoted to working for peace in the nuclear age, is housed at the Reconstructionist Rabbinical College in Philadelphia and is engaged in speaking about sane defense strategies in an authentically Jewish voice.

Of course, not every traditional Jewish value is acceptable to contemporary American Jews. We have much to gain by incorporating contemporary mores into the Jewish civilization—with regard to the equal role of women, the decent treatment of homosexuals, or support for the disabled. Nor does the Jewish tradition ever speak in an unambiguous voice. The various embodiments of that tradition over the course of three thousand years of evolution allow for divergent interpretations. Israeli West Bank settlers and Peace Now activists alike make the claim that they are authentically Jewish. Committed American Jews can be found both in the "pro-choice" and "pro-life" camps on the issue of abortion. We do not maintain that authentic Jews must adopt one political view to the exclusion of all others. Rather, we suggest that both the Jewish community and American society have much to gain when committed Jews study their tradition in order to apply its insights to contemporary issues.

Jews and Christians in America

With the recent upsurge of interest in prayer in schools and the return of nativity scenes to public places, more Jews have begun to feel uneasy, revising their view that America is a secular and hospitable society. They have focused on the fact that most Americans are Christian, and have begun to assume that Christianity is the true religion of America, and that the Jews are therefore, at the least, peripheral.

As Reconstructionists, we have no quarrel with the right—and responsibility—of other Americans to introduce their own religiously derived values and perspectives into public-policy debates. It is precisely such behavior that we advocate for Jews, as part of the pluralistic model for unity in diversity.

Yet, bringing religious perspectives into the public arena must not conflict with the right of religious groups to be different. When religious groups seek to pass legislation concerning matters about which we lack a consensus, then influence becomes control, and the rights of the minority are undermined or denied. The attempt to legislate religious perspectives, and to claim a consensus where one does not exist, is destructive to the values of pluralism and mutual respect.

It is urgent that we initiate and support intergroup dialogue as a way to build bridges of understanding between Jews and other groups who share these concerns. We rejoice that the relationship between blacks and Jews is being revived. We continue in our common efforts with like-minded Christians who also advocate separation of church and state, and who share our dedication to preserving a pluralistic society where the right to be different is respected. It is precisely through open communication and political action that we can overcome threats to the American values we hold to be precious.

Changing Jewish Views of America's Promise

Over the last few decades, the idealistic view of American democracy has come under assault from a variety of perspectives. In the sixties, the civil rights movement and resistance to the Vietnam War made Americans more aware of the existence of poverty, racial injustice, and American militarism. It thus became more difficult to maintain an unambiguous patriotism that views America as an unsullied beacon of freedom. Even more important, in light of the failure of Western democracies to prevent and adequately to combat the Holocaust, in light of the environmental hazards and the nuclear threat to which modern science and technology have led, and in light of the growing recognition that life in secular, prosperous America fails to meet adequately many of our spiritual needs, many would question Kaplan's enthusiastic embrace of American culture.

Fifty years ago, Kaplan was engaged in an attempt to convince recently arrived Jews that, in Americanizing and thus in adopting American values, they need not abandon their Jewish heritage. Thus, he stressed the coincidence of American and Jewish values. Today, now that we have Americanized, it is clear that the values and world view of the two civilizations are not and cannot be identical. To be sure, they are complementary—it is possible for a committed Jew to be integrated into American life. Where the burden once was to become more American, living in two civilizations now requires Jews to work at becoming more Jewish.

As we continue to develop the Jewish tradition in ways that speak to contemporary people living in two civilizations, a certain amount of caution is required. We do not want to reduce Judaism to those few aspects of the tradition that can be seamlessly reconstructed to agree with contemporary values. Jewish tradition should rather be regarded as a needed corrective to the materialism, competition, rootlessness, and alienation that seems to come with contemporary secular culture. As we can be enriched as Jews through our immersion in contemporary culture, even more can we, as Americans, enrich our lives by turning to the treasures of the Jewish tradition and to the wealth of contemporary Jewish creativity both in Israel and in the Diaspora. Living in two civilizations should be understood clearly as a delicate balance in which we give and take from two competing but mutually inclusive systems without subordinating one to the other. Incremental assimilation is undesirable because it cuts Jews off from the tradition's resources—resources that are not available to them as Americans alone.

Reconstructionism Around the World

The Reconstructionist focus on living in two civilizations was created out of the experience of Jews living in the United States. Nonetheless, the model may be (and has been) used for Jews living in other countries and cultures. The influence of Reconstructionist thought has been felt especially in Canada, where there are active Reconstructionist groups in Montreal and Toronto. The goal of living comfortably in a society that allows Jews the freedom to be both part and apart applies to the Canadian scene, in some ways even more than to the United States.

Reconstructionism's influence has also been felt in the Caribbean. In Curaçao, two congregations, one Reform and one traditional, were united into one Reconstructionist group following a Kaplanian model. Refusenik Jews in the Soviet Union have become aware of Reconstructionism, as a large number of our rabbis and leaders have chosen to visit and bring support to Soviet Jewry. The "two civilizations" problem is relevant in every secular nation.

Above all, Reconstructionists have been involved in creating alternative forms of religious expression in Israel. The issue of living in multiple civilizations exists for the Israeli population as well. They must understand the varied Jewish cultures with which they live, as well as the Western and Near Eastern settings that influence their lives and fates. There is a congregation in Jerusalem, *Mevakshei Derekh* (Seekers of the Way), which was founded on Kaplanian principles.

In Israel, Jews can explore "living in two civilizations" in a unique fashion. Since Judaism serves as the dominant influence there, Israeli Jews must meet the challenges of being in power, of granting other minorities the rights to explore their own civilizations, and of avoiding the creation of a state interpretation of Judaism that stifles other interpretations and new ideas.

Moreover, it is in Israel that the challenge of integrating the traditional aspects of Judaism with contemporary values is most pressing. However one defines the Jewishness of the Israeli state, the challenge of applying the tradition to a contemporary society remains an ongoing task.

CHAPTER SIX

ZION AS A SPIRITUAL CENTER

The Reconstructionist understanding of the civilizational character of Judaism predictably has led us to Zionist conclusions from the very outset. If Judaism is recognized as the civilization of the Jewish people, then there is no denying the particular attachment of our people to the Land of Israel—the site of our origins and genesis, and the focus of our hopes and ideals through the millenia. Kaplan and his associates were supporters of the Zionist cause decades before American Jewry reached its current consensus. They worked for the Zionist cause while other Jews declared that America was their Zion, denied that Israel could emerge before the coming of the Messiah, or worried that Jews would be accused of being disloyal if they allied themselves with another nation.

While he articulated the possibilities for modern Jews who live in two civilizations, Kaplan was aware that Jewish civilization could flourish completely only in a society in which it is primary. He was convinced that Zionist efforts to reestablish a Jewish presence in the land of Israel were central to Jewish renewal.

Spiritual Zionism

In the first part of the twentieth century, before the establishment of the State of Israel, the Zionist movement was divided. Political Zionists emphasized the need for a Jewish state to which Jews could go to escape anti-Semitic discrimination. A Jewish state could normalize the status of the Jewish people by making us like all other peoples. Spiritual or cultural Zionists, by contrast, emphasized the need for a return to the Land, so that Jewish culture could flourish in a Jewish environment and so that the values of our tradition could develop in a healthy, modern setting. It was with the latter, the spiritual Zionist camp, that Kaplan was associated. Its foremost spokesperson, Ahad Ha'am, was one of Kaplan's most significant teachers.

Ahad Ha'am rejected the stifling atmosphere of Russia, where he lived. He dreamed of a society in the land then known as Palestine where Jews could use the Hebrew language to express the nuances of their insights, where the Jewish heritage could be studied

47

through the prism of the modern outlook, where legal restraints would not limit careers or education, and where a new society could develop naturally out of the collective experiences of Jews in their own land. Its culture would be authentically loyal to its heritage, yet thoroughly contemporary in applying that heritage to a modern society. Its cultural renaissance could be a beacon radiating Jewish renewal to communities across the globe, and the foundations it laid would ensure that Judaism would make an invigorated transition to the modern era.

Deeply influenced by the vision of Aḥad Ha'am, Kaplan was outspoken in his support for the Jewish upbuilding of Palestine. The dream began to take shape as Hebrew became a spoken language again, reborn after two thousand years of use only for study and prayer. Scholars began to study biblical history. The Hebrew University became a center for the study of Judaica. Folk music and dance were created, incorporating biblical themes. Agricultural settlements and trade unions were founded on the basis of the conscious adaptation of prophetic and rabbinic ideals to the economy of a modern society.

Other Jewish Centers

Kaplan differed from cultural Zionism, however, in one significant respect. While he agreed with Aḥad Ha'am that Israeli culture would be the center of the Jewish renaissance, he believed that Jewish centers in the Diaspora should influence that center as well as be influenced by it. Each Jewish community had developed its own customs and viewpoints through interdependent connections with others over the last two thousand years. So, too, could the interaction of American Jewry, with its distinctive environment, enrich Jewish civilization as a whole. He rejected the political Zionists' *shelilat hagolah* (the negation of the Diaspora), affirming that Israel was not the only site in which Judaism could flourish.

Kaplan understood that, for American Jews, America is home, and that its Jewish renaissance ought thus to occur in the context of life in two civilizations. While others implored Western Jews to make *aliyah* for the sake of Jewish survival, Kaplan's position remained that Jews who do not face persecution will opt for life in Israel only when it offers them a credible promise of a fulfilling Jewish life. His focus remained, therefore, on the need for Israel to develop a reconstructed *Jewish* culture and ethos.

What is a Jewish State?

Despite the reticence of most committed Western Jews to make *aliyah*, Israel remains central to our loyalty and self-definition. In supporting Israel, we do more than contribute to the security and welfare of our fellow Jews. We also affirm our vigilance against the machinations of anti-Semites. And we pledge our solidarity to the Zionist political programs that are based upon taking our fate into our own hands. Morever, nearly four decades after the "miracle" of statehood and the War of Independence, we are still thrilled to think that biblical archaeology can be the passion of a nation, that a modern university would devote its computer facilities to the accessioning of rabbinic responsa, that *Adon Olam* can top the music charts on the radio. Furthermore, we have come to depend on the resources of Israeli scholars and educators for our own Jewish enrichment.

In the first years of the state, many Israelis were content to claim that theirs was the only Jewish community capable of surviving and worthy of surviving. In those years, Reconstructionists articulated the hope that productive relationships might be established between Israeli and other Jewish cultural centers. Today, Israelis see more clearly that Israelis are Jews too, and that all Jews share a common fate and hope. The current debate in Israel is rather about what it means to be a Jewish state.

Competing Visions

That debate can be summarized with reference to two issues. First, the original Zionist program was, to a certain extent, utopian and even messianic. By returning to the Jewish soil after shriveling on alien turf, the Jewish spirit would be revived. The society to be formed would be based on such ancient biblical ideals as justice and true community, and thus the normalization of the Jewish people in its own land would serve the community of nations as a model to be emulated. Israelis would teach others how to drain swamps and make deserts bloom, how to form a prosperous and democratic society out of diverse population groups.

The utopia envisioned by pre-state Zionists has been modified by reality. The problems Israel faces are staggering—unremitting Arab hostility, enormous defense budgets, cultural conflicts between Ashkenazim and Sephardim, and the relentless temptations of popular Western culture. In place of the original vision, we now witness the growth of a new Israeli messianism—one which rejects the Israeli founders' dream as "Western" and seeks to replace it with a fundamentalist Orthodox vision of Israel as the instrument of the divine will. The Jewish people, it claims, were given title to the Land by God in biblical times, and it is therefore unconditionally ours. Our victories are divinely willed, and our enemies are God's enemies. If Palestinian claims stand in the way of our possession of God's gift, then we may disregard their rights for the sake of heaven.

Reconstructionists, for all of our devotion to Israel, stand adamantly opposed to this fundamentalist, pseudomessianic revival. We believe that the reestablishment of the State of Israel resulted not from the supernatural intervention of God into history, but rather from the tireless and idealistic efforts of Zionist pioneers. We remain committed to a vision of an Israeli society that, applying ancient Jewish values to new circumstances, treats all of its citizens justly and seeks peace with its neighbors whenever possible. We turn to Kaplan's formulation of Judaism as a religion of ethical nationhood as we support those Israelis who are devoted to these traditional Jewish values that have preserved us through the centuries.

Responsibility to Non-Jews

The second area of debate concerns the responsibility that Jews—in Israel and elsewhere—bear to non-Jews. The founders of the Israeli state were committed to the establishment of a society that would differ from others in its approach to international relations. Israel would, of course, develop the capacity to defend efficiently the lives and safety of its citizens. Its wars, however, would only be wars of defense, its military campaigns designed thoughtfully to minimize unnecessary civilian casualties, its readiness to negotiate for peace constant, even in the face of relentlessly hostile neighbors.

Even before 1948, some Zionist factions attacked this commitment, believing it to be based on an unrealistic view of the world. Jews had always been prey to their enemies, and the primary contribution of an independent Jewish state would be its ability, at long last, to fight those enemies on equal terms. This view has been reinforced continually—by the Holocaust, by the silence of the Western nations in the weeks preceding the Six Day War, and by the aid and comfort that Palestinian terrorists have found in the capitals of the civilized world. All such events are taken to confirm the view that the Jews have no reliable friends and that our exclusive responsibility is to strengthen our capacity to foil the designs of our foes.

Most Reconstructionists take their stand with the vision of the Israeli founders. The long-term viability of the Jewish state depends, we believe, on its loyalty to traditional ethical principles. The lesson of the Holocaust is not only that we must be vigilant in our own defense, but also that we must oppose injustice and cruelty no matter who is the victim. It is as a religion of ethical nationhood that the State of Israel and Jewish civilization as a whole will weather our challenges. Judaism must stand for an enriching and ennobling way of life if it is to be worth defending indefinitely. A program advocating survival for its own sake preserves the shell while allowing our precious core to slip away. Israel can demand support both from Jews and from nations only as a democratic state that is simultaneously a loyal ally and a strong upholder of our highest ideals.

Religion in Israel

The Labor Zionist program was formed by pioneering activists who rebelled against the Orthodoxy of their Eastern European origins. Thus, they formulated a secular model for the Israeli state that spurned not only Orthodox religion but all Jewish religion. The 2,000 year history of the Jewish people in the Diaspora initially was ignored, and Judaism as religion was abandoned to the Orthodox rabbinate.

As a result, the quality of Jewish life in Israel continues to suffer. Israelis continue to define themselves either as *dati'im* (Orthodox) or *hiloni'im* (secular), with little room in the middle for a non-Orthodox, liberal religious expression. The complexity of Israeli coalition politics has exacerbated this problem, because it has allowed Orthodox political parties to bargain for power beyond their numbers— power that they have used to thwart attempts to develop non-Orthodox religious alternatives.

It is ironic that a diversity of Jewish religious alternatives has been so limited in the Jewish state. Israelis are prevented by state law and coalition agreements, for example, from using public transportation or attending concerts on Shabbat or acting in other ways that offend Orthodox sensibilities. They are restrained by those same regulations from developing alternate forms of Shabbat observance that would violate the halakhah of the Orthodox. Orthodox synagogues, yeshivot, and school systems routinely receive financial support from the government. Non-Orthodox synagogues most commonly are left to their own devices. The message is clear: the only acceptable form of Judaism in Israel is Orthodox Judaism. Faced with that alternative, most Israelis choose not to define themselves as religious.

This explains why the only non-Orthodox alternatives in Israel are foreign imports—Reform, Conservative, and Progressive alternatives that are supported from abroad. The Jerusalem congregation *Mevakshei Derekh* (Seekers of the Way), founded on Kaplanian principles, had to meet in a high school for two decades before the municipality could be prodded into granting it a parcel of land on which to build. In contrast to Orthodox synagogues, most of the funds for construction of a synagogue-center have had to be raised privately. It is primarily Western immigrants, aware that there are meaningful religious alternatives to Orthodoxy, who are the mainstay of these small movements.

But the potential is there. Israelis, no less than other Jews across the globe, confront the challenges of modernity. They, too, are in need of the spiritual treasures of our tradition as they deal with neighbors and cope with the stresses of contemporary life. Secular Israeli society itself provides them with what diaspora Jews lack: a schooling in Jewish history and Israeli culture; new folkways dealing with the Shabbat and holidays; and an effortless immersion in Jewish language, landscape, and lore. But Israel has insufficient opportunities for spiritual exploration and for plumbing our tradition for fresh ideas about how to confront personal and national moral questions. Israelis who are uncomfortable with Orthodoxy need new Israeli forms of religious life.

Reconstructionists tend to feel a close kinship with those Israelis —the noted novelist Amos Oz, for example—who are moving towards a reclamation of Judaism as a *religion* of ethical nationhood, towards a revivification of Jewish religious life in a liberal, sexually egalitarian, naturalistic way. It is not for us to prescribe the forms that an indigenous and liberal Israeli Judaism should take. We maintain our solidarity, however, with those struggling for a pluralistic Jewish society in which religious options are not constrained by the dictates of the Orthodox rabbinate. Pluralism is as crucial in Israel as it is in America or Europe.

Criticism of Israeli Policies

For many years, awestruck by the monumental achievement of the builders of the Jewish state, diaspora Jews idealized the state and believed it could do no wrong. As the new state struggled to build a viable economy and to overcome international hostility, Jews around the world believed that their role was to serve as Israel's unconditional defenders. No one could understand the meaning of Israel as well as Jews; only we understood that the existence of the State of Israel needed no justification.

Since the 1967 war and especially since the 1973 war, however, Jewish communities have debated the appropriateness of Jewish criticism of Israeli policies. The Jewish critic may have noble intentions but should be wary lest loving criticisms become ammunition in the hands of those who wish to delegitimize the State of Israel.

Reconstructionist Jews are sensitive to these concerns; those Jews who issue public statements and hold news conferences must weigh their positive effects against their potential dangers. We do not believe, however, that the solidarity of the Jewish people requires that we mute our criticisms in fear of what the gentiles will say. The issues that are debated, often vociferously, within Israeli society—the Jewish settlement of the West Bank, Orthodox hegemony, Ashkenazi-Sephardi relations, questions of Jewish identity, the status of Israeli Arabs—are too important to the fate of all Jews to be left to Israelis alone. It is therefore our view that non-Israeli Jews must insist that their voices be included in those debates. Just as Israel's victories since 1947 have given us new-found pride, so can its moral character diminish or reinvigorate our moral self-understanding.

Zionists Can Live in the Diaspora

Israelis are less adamant today than ever before in insisting that Jews in the Diaspora must make *aliyah* to be truly loyal to the Jewish state. One still hears the claim, however, that Jewish life in North America, for example, is doomed to failure—because of the inevitability of anti-Semitism and/or because of the irreversibility of progressive assimilation. The common Israeli reading of history is that all golden ages of Jewish life in the Diaspora have ended tragically before, and that diaspora Jews who ignore this long series of precedents are self-deluding.

Reconstructionists reject the claim that living in Israel is the only possible way to ensure Jewish survival. We are firmly convinced of the need for the Jewish state—both as a haven for the oppressed and as the optimal site of Jewish cultural and spiritual renewal in our time. As Jewish civilization has been enriched by the diversity of Jewish communities in the past, so today do both Israeli and diaspora Jews have much to gain by developing in independent but interrelated ways.

We do not regard the State of Israel as the complete realization of the age-old Jewish ideal of Zion. Israelis, no less than diaspora Jews, are moderns struggling with the meaningful adaptation of the Jewish tradition in a new era. They, like us, are fallible. They are locked into a particular socio-political circumstance in which they must be relentlessly vigilant against military attack and in which their interaction with the non-Jewish world is necessarily limited.

North American Jews live in very different circumstances that, for the foreseeable future, will allow us the unprecedented opportunity to develop as Jews while being intimately connected with non-Jews in an open, pluralistic setting. While the future cannot be foretold, we certainly hope that both modern Jewish experiments will continue to flourish, contributing new chapters to Jewish history and supporting each other.

The challenge before North America Zionists is thus neither to convince our most committed people that a full Jewish life is possible only in Israel, nor to sound the trumpets of doom about our future. It is rather to develop creative programs that bring us in closer touch with our Israeli cousins. Our philanthropic generosity and the strength of the United Jewish Appeal are important indications of our commitment that need to be broadened. Subsidized summer programs for teens and adults, educational tours, and work-study programs that bring diaspora Jews into close touch with Israelis; opportunities for study institutes, organized programs facilitating sabbatical exchanges with Israelis—all of these ideas and others should be given priority by the North American Jewish community. Their success cannot be measured by the number of participants persuaded by them to make *aliyah*, but rather in the enrichment they provide for the quality of our Jewish lives. The link between Israeli and diaspora Jews can enrich and strengthen both.

In the end, both the land of Israel and its people will remain central to the consciousness of committed Jews everywhere. Our fate is linked inextricably to theirs, and we look to them for leadership. Reconstructionists, however, maintain that, in addition to basking in the rays that come forth from Jerusalem, diaspora Jews must also generate light, for our own illumination and that of Israelis as well. Only in partnership can we fulfill the destiny of the Jewish people.

CHAPTER SEVEN

WHO IS A JEW?

An essential task for every group is to define who belongs to it. Given Judaism's long history and the countless migrations of the Jewish people, it is no wonder that our criteria for membership have fluctuated through the ages. At times, we have had very rigid boundaries, strictly limiting those people who could be defined as Jews by birth and conversion. At other times, we have been more fluid, and special categories existed for "fellow travelers" within the Jewish community.

For many centuries we have had a very precise definition of who is a Jew. According to this definition, a person is Jewish if he or she is born of a Jewish mother or if he or she undergoes a process of conversion. This conversion process includes a lengthy period of studying Jewish culture, beliefs, and practices; ritual immersion for women and men; ritual circumcision for men; and examination by a *bet din* (Jewish court of three) that determines the candidate's commitment to living an observant Jewish life.

Today there are many people living Jewish lives who do not meet these criteria. Some were born to a Jewish father, but not to a Jewish mother. Some are married to Jews and raise Jewish children, but have never converted. Others were converted to Judaism by rabbis who did not insist on *all* the halakhic criteria of conversion—for example, omitting ritual circumcision for adult males, not insisting that the convert lead a totally observant life, or accepting people for conversion for the sake of marriage. Still others converted to Judaism in keeping with halakhah but are not recognized by the Orthodox because their conversions weren't witnessed by a *bet din* composed of Orthodox Jews. Some have had their Jewish identity questioned because they grew up in Ethiopia in a divergent Jewish tradition, or in the Soviet Union where Jewish practices were prohibited, making their lineage difficult to trace.

The Orthodox rabbinate has gone so far as to define these people out of the Jewish fold, requiring them to convert under Orthodox auspices if they wish to be recognized as Jews. Other rabbis, Reconstructionists among them, take a different approach. We respond by recognizing the need to broaden the definition of who is a Jew to include people who are living as committed members of the Jewish community. Naturally, these decisions are of paramount concern for the Jewish people. The Reconstructionist approach to the problem of Jewish definition is thus indicative of our approach to the resolution of the crisis of Judaism in our age.

Reconstructionist Conversion

Reconstructionists are committed to the ritual of conversion. We feel it is important for anyone not born of a Jewish parent to undergo this symbolic rite of passage so that they may publicly proclaim their connection to the community.

While the Reconstructionist rabbi who instructs a prospective convert clearly differs from his/her Orthodox colleague in terms of the *content* of instruction, the *process* is essentially the same. We, too, insist on a significant period of study—but incorporate more than learning about how to be an observant Jew, though that is included, too. We want those people who join us to feel a sense of belonging. Converts to Judaism through the Reconstructionist method study history, observance, and beliefs, but they also learn to make choices. They are connected to the community through relationships with others who have chosen Judaism, and they are located in a Jewish community of which they can become a part after the conversion ceremony.

All Reconstructionist Jews by choice go through a process that includes ritual immersion for men and women, circumcision for men (unless the psychological or physical difficulty is too great), and a *bet din*—a discussion with three knowledgeable Jews (at least one of them a rabbi), who welcome the convert through a sympathetic dialogue. Many Reconstructionist communities have added a public ceremony of welcome, sometimes held on *Shavuot* because of its connection to the biblical story of Ruth, the paradigmatic Jew by choice.

Matrilineal and Patrilineal Descent

The Reconstructionist movement's policy is that conversion is unnecessary for a person born of one Jewish parent, mother or father, when that child is raised and educated as a Jew. In the first centuries of our era—*only* eighteen or nineteen centuries ago—the Tannaitic rabbis decided that Jewish identity would be transmitted only through the mother (matrilineal descent). Current research indicates that before that time, identity had been transmitted through the father. When the rabbis made that reversal, they lived in a Roman empire in which the matrilineal principle was the norm for all matters of personal status. Moreover, they were addressing a Jewish community in which a Jewish mother was a virtual guarantee that a child would be Jewish, and a non-Jewish mother similarly would determine that her children would not be Jewish.

The Reconstructionist movement, since 1968, has recognized the Jewishness of the child of a Jewish father and a non-Jewish mother when that child is raised and educated as a Jew (patrilineal descent). We have done so for a number of reasons that we believe are compelling.

First, we believe that the circumstances of the open society render the traditional norm obsolete. Two millenia ago, when the rare intermarriage occurred, the children followed the religion of the mother. Thus, the rabbis' matrilineal principle was not an edict pronounced in a vacuum; it responded to the social realities of the time. Today, that is not the case. Jewish children are being raised by Jewish fathers and non-Jewish mothers.

The effects of this discrepancy between Jewish law and the de facto realities are, we believe, injurious to the health of Jewish civilization. Children who have been raised as Jews are sometimes forced to undergo halakhic conversion prior to their bar/bat mitzvah ceremonies, thus communicating to them that Jewishness is a matter of formalistic—almost magical—ritual, rather than the living of a Jewish life. Rabbis who are otherwise sensitively inclined often find themselves compelled to uphold the dictates of tradition no matter what the emotional cost. Divorced Jewish fathers find that they have no legal basis to ask the civil courts to allow their children to receive a Jewish education. This illustrates that the rigid upholding of halakhah in this case can be counterproductive. It sanctifies a human, historically-conditioned rabbinic ruling, whose consequences were unforeseeable to those rabbis. It denies the evolving nature of Jewish civilization.

Second, the matrilineal principle is based on assumptions about gender roles that are no longer viable. It is no longer automatic in our society that the mother is the primary provider of child care. Jewish fathers are also involved in raising their children in ways unheard of in previous eras. While most of the gender-related disabilities imposed by the Jewish tradition are suffered by women, in this case it is the father who suffers. Inasmuch as we are dedicated to the removal of all such disabilities and to the cultivation of a community in which men and women can choose their roles freely, patrilineal descent must be restored alongside matrilineal descent.

Third, we believe that Jewish identity is cultivated by living a Jewish life, and is not something that is automatically inherited. At a time when having *two* Jewish parents is no guarantee that a child will be raised as a Jew, it is counterproductive to insist that a person raised as a Jew and identifying as a Jew is not a Jew because his/her mother did not convert before the birth. We understand rituals as deriving their power and efficacy from the way they symbolize real transactions. Thus, conversion rituals "work" when they express an actual entry of a non-Jew into our community. When they are imposed arbitrarily, however, in the belief that the edicts of generations long gone must be obeyed, those rituals degenerate into rote performances.

Fourth, we are dedicated to the reconstruction of Jewish life because we believe that there are countless Jews who are alienated from traditional forms of Jewish life but who are seeking means of spiritual fulfillment. Many of those Jews have already chosen non-Jewish spouses or will do so in the future. Already, intermarried Jews represent a sizable percentage of the North American Jewish population. We believe that a reconstructed Judaism can meet the needs of many of those Jews. In our open society, it is easy to leave the Jewish community. It is therefore imperative that we avoid increasing the difficulty of the return of those who are so inclined.

Finally, we believe that a revitalized Jewish civilization must be sensitive and humanitarian if it is to be worth preserving. It enriches our lives because it provides us with insights into the human condition, with means of expressing our deepest aspirations, and with a community of Jews with whom we can share our quest for meaning and integration. We value the Jewish tradition because it offers us the wisdom of past generations that helps us to achieve these ends. We do not value all of it unconditionally. Quite to the contrary, we reject the interpretation of Judaism that insists it is a static system to which Jews must submit, relinquishing their autonomy. When the matrilineal principle is used in this way, we believe it must be changed.

Intermarriage

North American Jews today live in an open society. We share much in common with our non-Jewish neighbors, including the assumption that individuals should have the liberty to choose the course of their lives and that marriage partners should be selected based on loving relationships. Yet we want our children to marry Jews—to pass on their Jewish heritage to yet another generation. Often, these values are in conflict.

We could, of course, withdraw from the open society by choosing *aliyah* to Israel or by screening out the secular society as Hasidim do. Or we could continue to recite the Mourner's Kaddish over a son or daughter who has intermarried, marking him or her as one who is leaving the fold. That these options are not advocated seriously is an indication of our widespread acceptance of the open society.

For several generations, we relied on the slowness of Jewish acculturation. Jews may have been equal under the law, but we remained different from our non-Jewish neighbors. Living in Jewish neighborhoods and suburbs, sending our children to Jewish camps and teen and college programs, our insistence that Jews marry only Jews was largely effective. Even in the early 1960s, an intermarrying Jew was most likely one whose action demonstrated his or her conscious and active desire to abandon Jewish identity.

Today, however, that is no longer an accurate assumption. Jews regularly marry non-Jews while simultaneously maintaining positive identification as Jews. Studies show that it is most often the case that they choose non-Jewish partners who are lapsed and uncommitted Christians, and that it is often the case that these mixed couples want to raise Jewish children. Even when they are indifferent to their Jewishness, they are no more indifferent than large numbers of Jews who are married to Jews.

Faced with these new circumstances, we seek new solutions. We view our primary responsibility as revitalizing Jewish life. In so doing, even indifferent Jews—no matter whom they have married— will want to join us in our quest to Judaize our lives. And when we are faced with the common case of intermarried couples and families who want to be involved in Jewish life, we believe the sensible course is not only to welcome them, but to seek them out. Thus, Reconstructionist groups across the continent are involved in active outreach—sponsoring courses introducing Jews to Judaism, facilitating peer groups in which mixed couples can share their distinctive predicaments, developing communal forms of Jewish celebrations that help Jews become familiar with the tradition's treasures. Our goal is to bring increasing numbers of Jews—and their spouses and children—into the Jewish orbit.

For too long, the Jewish community has focused its efforts on convincing the non-Jewish partner to become Jewish before the wedding. This has been the case because rabbis and families have not wanted to face the question of the mixed couple's wedding ceremony. Jews regularly are told that if they really care about Judaism, they should insist upon their spouse's conversion before the wedding.

This is not always a wise focus of our concerns for several reasons. Countless couples have become embittered and hostile to the Jewish community because they met indifferent and even hostile rabbinic responses to their requests for rabbinic officiation. Studies show that significant numbers of non-Jewish spouses convert years after the wedding. The period preceding the wedding, when the couple is involved in creating a relationship independent of their respective families, is often the worst possible time to bring uninvited pressure to bear upon them.

While the large majority of Reconstructionist rabbis do not officiate at mixed-marriage ceremonies, all Reconstructionist rabbis are committed to making themselves available for counseling and guidance. The decision not to officiate is based on the belief that it is inauthentic to use Jewish symbols in a ceremony that unites a Jew and a non-Jew, and on the view that the rabbi is perceived as a living Jewish symbol. Nevertheless, Reconstructionist rabbis convey to couples that they are interested in working with them to explore their Jewish options and will not pass negative and hostile judgments. Under appropriate circumstances, some will attend civil ceremonies and, although not officiating, will offer remarks welcoming the couple's intentions to create a Jewish home. Reconstructionist groups are open to the participation and membership of mixed couples.

We adopt this spirit of welcome in our conviction that we have no basis to stand in judgment. Those who condemn intermarriage as if it were sinful really are condemning the fruits of the open society to which they are otherwise dedicated. It is not true that intermarriages have a higher rate of divorce or that it is always the case that a Jew would be better off marrying a Jew than a non-Jew. Until we face those facts, we are likely to miss the opportunity to help peripheral Jews return to the community and tradition. Our task is thus not to condemn the intermarried, but rather to make Judaism compelling.

Such a welcoming attitude leads us to uncharted terrain. It challenges us to consider the roles of the unconverted partners. In many Reconstructionist congregations, they are members and participants in Jewish rituals. They generally do not serve as presidents of congregations, and they do not receive the honor of being called to the Torah. Yet their active presence challenges us to find ways of including them in our definition of membership in the Jewish community. It also enables them to feel included and respected by the Jewish community, making official conversion more attractive.

The Unity of the Jewish People

Many Jews—including many Reconstructionist Jews—are concerned about the danger of schism. Now that Reconstructionist and Reform Jews accept the patrilineal principle, and non-Jewish spouses who have not officially converted are welcomed in, our definition of Jewish identity departs from that of more traditional Jews who are now proclaiming that, without halakhic conversion, they will not allow their children to marry ours.

Let it be stated clearly at the outset that our intentions are not schismatic. We advise parents that a patrilineally descended child will not be recognized as Jewish by halakhic authorities, and we facilitate the formal conversion of infants when parents so desire. We maintain our devotion to the ideal of a Jewish community that is united despite its diversity.

We are faced, however, with an Orthodox community that does not even accept the conversions non-Orthodox rabbis do perform according to halakhic procedure, merely because those rabbis perform them. They seek to deny us the right to make any definition of who is a Jew, claiming that authority for themselves alone. But the issue runs deeper. At stake is the very survival of the Jewish people. We adamantly reject the version of Jewish history that suggests that there has always existed a normative, halakhic Judaism that has survived unchanged despite the challenges of Jewish heretics in every generation. A careful look at Jewish history reveals the fact that Jews have been divided in *every* generation. Every period of our history has been witness to competing interpretations of Judaism, whose advocates condemned one another. It has never been possible, in advance, to determine which group would emerge victorious to tell the tale. The only certainty has been that the victorious faction—incorporating aspects of its competitor's program and altered by that very competition—has portrayed the alternatives in retrospect as heresy.

Any serious attempt to account for the survival of the Jewish people must include the resilience of Jewish civilization—its remarkable ability to adapt to new conditions by developing new forms and reinterpreting once sacred beliefs. It has never been the case, however, that the most effective means of adaptation could be known in advance. In fact, we must assume that most innovations have not survived or even been recorded for posterity.

As we face the unprecedented challenges to Judaism of our ever more rapidly changing world, it is imperative that we be bold. We cannot be certain which of our reinterpretations will survive. We can be certain, however, that Jewish civilization will survive as a vital way of life only if it continues to adapt. In North America, that means that Jews living in an open society must be offered an interpretation of Judaism that will facilitate their becoming more involved. In such circumstances, we believe that the rigid adherence to halakhic forms—themselves once developed innovatively to meet past challenges—is a recipe for doom. Embracing the open society, we are committed to cultivating a Jewish renaissance that will welcome all Jews who are interested in participating.

CHAPTER EIGHT

WOMEN AND JUDAISM: A CASE STUDY OF THE RECONSTRUCTIONIST APPROACH

The best way to appreciate the methods and goals of the Reconstructionist philosophy is to examine how they function in Jewish life today. One way to approach that examination is to study a particular issue in Jewish life. No issue better lends itself to this task than does the changed and changing role of Jewish women. An examination of the steps Reconstructionist Judaism has taken over the past fifty years underscores how the major concepts of Reconstructionist thinking can be put into practice.

It must be said at the outset that the women's issue would not be an issue for us if we did not live in two civilizations; for it is in the secular civilization that changes in women's roles have been initiated. It was in the 1920s that the women's suffrage movement gained prominence, raising the issue of women's equality and personhood. Aware of this trend, Kaplan strongly advocated that Judaism keep up with those changes in perception, both from a pragmatic and a moral point of view: pragmatic, because many women would lose interest in Jewish life if they were excluded from it in the public realm; moral, because the equality of all persons is a value espoused by the democratic tradition that Kaplan wished to introduce into Jewish life in new and unprecedented ways.

Of course, that is not to say that the position of women in Jewish life was static prior to Kaplan's time. Throughout Jewish history women were subject to varying levels of economic, social, political, and religious disabilities. Most frequently, the status of women in Jewish life fluctuated with the status of women in those civilizations with which the Jews came into contact.

The changes that have taken place in most recent times, however, are qualitatively different. For the first time, women themselves have sought to speak in their own voices, not allowing their roles and status to be defined for them by men. It is of no small consequence that Kaplan foresaw that this would happen as early as 1946 when he urged the Jewish woman to "demand the equality due her as a right to which she is fully entitled."

To achieve the inclusion of women, three different courses of action have been required. In some cases (for example, celebrating bat mitzvah, having *aliyot*, and becoming rabbis), the form and content of the ritual has been retained, and women have been included. In others (for example, birth ceremonies, marriage, and divorce), the form and/or the content of the ritual have been modified, so that the power of the traditional ceremony can be retained without subjecting women to disabilities. In still other cases (for example, liturgical language), the feminist critique of Judaism has led to a radical questioning of the very words we use and the actions we perform.

Bat Mitzvah

The first step was instituting bat mitzvah. Since late medieval times, the Jewish community had celebrated the bar mitzvah ceremony when boys attained the age of majority. No corresponding recognition or public ceremony existed for girls. This was the case for two reasons. First, the bar mitzvah ceremony took place in the synagogue, as the boy was called up to the Torah for the first time. Since it had become the tradition that women were not eligible to be called up to the Torah, the ceremony would not have made sense. Second, when a girl reached adulthood, that had significance in terms of her marriageability and a small number of other commandments related to holiday and home observance—and *not* for any other new role she would play in the performance of *public* rituals.

Had traditional Jewish society been interested in valuing or publicly celebrating the woman's role, a ceremony might have been developed around a girl's transition to puberty. Without this interest, it is not surprising that no such public celebration developed. And if women, acting outside the public domain, developed private celebrations, that, too, is lost to us—the activities of women were not of interest to the men who kept public records for posterity.

In Kaplan's era, bat mitzvah, which we take for granted, was unheard of. Long before, classical Reform Judaism had done away with the bar mitzvah ceremony as well. In Reform settings at that time, the Torah was not frequently read in public, and no one was called up to recite the Torah blessings. The traditionalists, on the other hand, had no notion that women's equality should be an issue within the context of Jewish life. In 1922, when Kaplan's eldest daughter Judith reached the age of twelve, it was decided that she would be called to the Torah at the Society for the Advancement of

Judaism. The event went on with little fanfare, but it was indeed a historic occasion.

That innovation in Jewish life would not have been possible had Kaplan not been looking for ways to give the past a vote but not a veto. In this case, Kaplan opted for retaining the form and content of the traditional ceremony, broadening its meaning to include young women.

The same approach was later taken with regard to other disabilities women faced in public Jewish ritual—being called to the Torah for an *aliyah* (to recite the blessing over the Torah upon its being read), being counted in a *minyan* (the ten who constitute a quorum for Jewish worship), and being counted as a witness for signing Jewish documents. These traditions are still meaningful, so there was no need to alter them radically; rather, there was a need to augment them by permitting women equal access to them, counting both women and men as part of the community that finds such actions meaningful. In Reconstructionist circles, women were taking this active role in ritual in the early 1950s, a generation before this became common elsewhere.

Women in the Rabbinate

Another example of giving women equal access to roles that previously were performed exclusively by men is the training of women to be rabbis. The Reconstructionist Rabbinical College opened its doors in 1968. During its first year, a woman (Sandy Eisenberg Sasso) applied and was accepted to begin her studies the following fall. Significant numbers of others followed in her footsteps, and by 1974, half of each entering class at the RRC was female. It is to the credit of the institution that woman students were treated as equals by faculty, administration, and by their male colleagues. It should also be noted that the RRC has been in the vanguard in opening full-time faculty and administrative posts to women.

Will the presence of women performing traditionally male roles radically alter Judaism? On one level, the answer is no, or at least no more than any other measure that increases the number of people who are eligible to take active roles in Jewish life.

Yet, in a deeper sense, women in public roles will make a profound difference. That a girl now can grow up assuming that she has a rightful, public place in the synagogue makes an enormous difference in the consciousness of children. Women may also bring different sensibilities to the rabbinate—making public such concerns as domestic violence, family planning, child-rearing, and human sexuality. Women undoubtedly will also bring a greater awareness of "sexism"—how power gets divided within institutional structures, often to the disadvantage of women.

Based on their feminist perspective, women may also concern themselves with the conduct of *all* human relationships and include *all* people who are considered marginal—restoring the ancient prophetic dream. This is the ultimate, if yet unrealized, potential of the changes which we began to initiate many years ago.

We believe that just as women's roles have been broadened, so men's roles must be broadened as well. If women are to take a more active role in public expressions of Judaism, so men's roles in the home and family must be enhanced. Only in this way can people freely and equally express what it means to them to be Jewish.

Initiating Baby Girls Into the Covenant

Other insights of feminism have led to more active reconstruction of the form and content of Jewish life. Unlike bar mitzvah, the *brit milah* (circumcision) for boys has no easy parallel for girls. While it was understood that boys would be entered into the covenant of the Jewish people eight days after birth with the sign of circumcision, there was no corresponding entrance of girls into the covenant or any other special public ceremony for them. Jewish feminists of all types have devoted much energy to creating ceremonies welcoming baby girls.

Those that have been created using the Reconstructionist perspective have paid a great deal of attention to the need to create *berakhot* (blessings) that reflect the understanding that women are part of the covenant of Israel. They have also sought symbolic acts to convey the power of circumcision—acts that express the deep psychological meaning of bringing a child into the world and into the Jewish community. The Reconstructionist perspective makes us particularly attuned to the aesthetics of the ceremony. Seeing Judaism as a civilization reminds us of the need to engage the artistic and cultural dimensions as well. Two Reconstructionist ceremonies using these insights were among the first created by Jewish feminists. One was by the first rabbinical couple, another by a group of Reform and Reconstructionist woman rabbis.

The first ceremony, written in 1974 by Rabbis Sandy and Dennis Sasso, is called *Brit Bnot Yisrael* (A Covenant for the Daughters of Israel). The following paragraph, to be recited by the parents, indicates its focus:

> We gather together on the Shabbat with family and friends to bring our daughter into the Covenant of the Jewish people. For millennia, the Shabbat has been a sign of covenantal commitment which has inspired generations of our people with the drive to creativity and the values of human dignity. Therefore, on this Shabbat we bring our daughter before this community that she may be linked with the Covenant of the people of Israel.

The nine woman rabbis who put together the second ceremony, *Brit Reḥitzah* (the Covenant of Washing) were searching for a symbol of covenant, and decided on washing the baby's feet, as they describe:

> The idea of water proved to be a compelling one. We wanted something ancient and Jewish, something without diversionary overtones, something physical and something meaningful vis-à-vis the event at hand: a welcoming into the covenant. We recalled that the Bible speaks of more than one covenant. In addition to the covenant with Abraham which is the basis of the *brit milah*, a covenant is also made with Noah after the flood. Surely, we would want to welcome the baby girl into that covenant as well, a covenant that potentially involves all of humanity. With Noah, we were once again drawn to water: the life-giving "Mayim Ḥayim," that had threatened to destroy, but now preserved human life. Water. Washing. Welcoming. . . . Someone remembered that when Abraham was recovering from his circumcision, he was visited by three angels of the Lord who promised him that his seed would continue and that Sarah would have a son. Abraham greeted these strangers with the gracious Middle Eastern sign of hospitality—he gave them water to wash their feet. What better way, then, for us to welcome our new members into the family of people and the family of Jews? Foot washing is gentle, loving, and ancient. It is also tangible and earthy: there is touching and splashing and the cry of the baby when first shocked by the cold water. Through this act, we hoped to help create a meaningful and memorable rite of passage. The

ritual grew, as you can see, organically and communally. The end product is not important. You may borrow it, adapt it, ignore it. What *is* important is that the process of creating Judaism is far from over. The committee hopes that others will continue the task. Judaism is too precious for us not to want it to grow.

Thus the form and content of the ceremony for welcoming baby girls into the world continues to develop dramatically, with various options offered to enable parents to involve themselves in this momentous event from the perspective of ritual.

Jewish Divorce

The same process of changing form and content has been necessary for Jewish divorce procedures. The essential problem here is that, traditionally, women are ineligible to initiate divorce proceedings. If a Jewish court cannot compel an unwilling husband to initiate a divorce, the woman cannot have another Jewish marriage. There are still cases today of *agunot*—women who find themselves barred from remarriage on this basis. The Reform movement solved this problem by permitting remarriage without a Jewish divorce. The Orthodox and Conservative movements look for legal loopholes to enable women to be remarried. In Reconstructionist thinking, giving the past a vote but not a veto in this case means preserving the idea of Jewish divorce. Judaism seeks to mark and hallow each part of the life cycle. If a marriage is worth marking as a Jewish event, there ought to be a corresponding Jewish event to end a marriage. But if we believe in equality, women must be allowed to initiate the proceedings when necessary.

In this case, however, raising the women's issue raised other questions and problems about the procedures entirely. Why should a man or a woman have to initiate divorce alone? If it is mutual decision, the procedure should be initiated by both parties. Just as in Reconstructionist weddings men and women give each other rings and pledge to be special for each other "according to the traditions of the people of Israel," so they should share as equals the responsibility for ending that status.

Reconstructionists have further been forced to question the text of the divorce document (*get*). The parallel to the wedding exists there too. The *ketubah* (marriage document) has been reconstructed in content, though not in form, to illustrate the new relationship that has evolved in marriage. Most frequently, Reconstructionist rabbis work with couples to write their own *ketubot* that articulate the goals they share for their relationship (such as sharing of household responsibilities, raising the children, or maintaining a high level of sensitivity to one another).

The language of the *get* has been reconstructed in a similar way to reflect the equality of the divorcing partners. In many cases, the scribe will be asked to write two documents, so that the man and woman truly divorce one another. In both marriage and divorce, the document form has been retained. Reconstructionists value having these written affirmations. They provide continuity with Jewish tradition while achieving intellectual honesty in content and acting as permanent records of the events.

The nature of the divorce ceremony is also in need of reconstruction. Unlike the wedding ceremony, in which the form itself carries deep meaning, the divorce proceeding was for many generations viewed exclusively as a legal procedure. Reconstructionists have perceived that, to achieve the level of meaning appropriate to divorce, a ceremony is needed that reflects the pain and sadness at divorce, the symbolic ending of a chapter in the life of the family, and the possibilities of new beginnings as well. To that end, several Reconstructionist rabbis have been involved in creating new ceremonies for divorce proceedings.

Changing divorce procedures raises questions of the unity of the Jewish people, an issue of great importance to Reconstructionists. In making these changes, we realize that we are acting in ways that more traditional segments of the community consider illegitimate. To be sure, Reconstructionists do not permit someone to become involved in an egalitarian divorce without making that person aware that it would not be accepted by all segments of our community. Because the Orthodox generally do not recognize any divorce except their own, however, there is no way to compromise concerning the form of the ceremony in order to achieve its universal acceptance.

Moreover, contemporary Jews continue to seek forms of Jewish expression that are meaningful and often find that traditional forms don't work. Thus, preserving ancient ways may not be a sensible alternative. Innovation is not evidence that we are less sensitive to the need for unity; rather, it is evidence of our commitment to meeting the needs of contemporary Jews. This in turn makes us more passionate about the need for pluralism on the part of all Jews as a cardinal principle of Jewish unity.

Liturgical Changes

There is no doubt that feminism has wrought major changes in Jewish life, calling upon us to ask questions that go beyond the equality of women to the fundamental level of the meaning of Judaism as it exists today. One example of that kind of questioning exists in the realm of liturgy. Of course, Jewish liturgy can be put to the egalitarian test. Our English translations are "sexist" in that they speak of "the brotherhood of men" and refer to individuals as "he," and to people as "mankind" or "men." That the Reconstructionist prayerbooks, composed over forty years ago, use these phrases only reminds us that the need to reconstruct exists in every generation. It is true that in those prayerbooks, as in all that preceded them, we pray to the "God of our Fathers, Abraham, Isaac, and Jacob" but omit our Mothers, Sarah, Rebeccah, Leah, and Rachel. This is a situation amenable to change without too much difficulty. These changes come under the category of bringing equality into the liturgical sphere. But feminists ask a deeper question: why do we always refer to God as He? Why are the vast majority of our metaphors for God—King, Shepherd, Father—set in male language?

As Reconstructionists, we have several ways of responding to this feminist challenge. The first possibility is to include feminine God language—to begin to refer to God also as She, Mother, strong and beautiful Woman. This way has several advantages. It gives women an opportunity to experience themselves as made in the image of God. It broadens our conception of how God works in the world. It challenges us to be clear that our anthropomorphic images are just that—that God can fit comfortably into all of them, yet can't be contained by any. So God can be addressed as He or She—reminding us that God is neither one.

Yet there is another Reconstructionist approach to this question. Perhaps feminism has come to remind us that our metaphors cannot approximate our concept of God. Perhaps God is best addressed as Power or Process. If so, we might think, with Rabbi Harold Schulweis, about reformulating some of our prayers to read *Berukhah ha-Elohut*, blessed is Godliness.

This does not imply that Reconstructionists reject male God language completely. We recognize the mythic power and the metaphorical truth of the traditional liturgy. The language of our ancient prayers resonates in ways that transcend literal intellectual affirmation. Thus, it is possible for some to accept feminist insights, avoiding idolatrous attachment to a literal male image of God while retaining traditional prayer forms.

Of course, these options are not mutually exclusive. Reconstructionists are now in the process of dealing with this issue, and a liturgy commission composed of men and women, congregants and rabbis, is grappling with these and other questions. Whatever the outcome now, we recognize that we will need to reconstruct the liturgy somewhat in each generation to keep pace with changing language, aesthetics, and knowledge. In doing so, we recognize the need to innovate not only by writing anew, but also by searching out the riches of the Jewish past.

By examining the changing roles of women and Judaism, we have explored a cross section of Reconstructionist thinking as it tackles a problem in its various manifestations. We now turn to questions of structure. What does it mean in reality to participate in the Reconstructionist community today? How do our institutions and platforms reflect our feelings, thoughts, and actions?

CHAPTER NINE

REORGANIZING THE JEWISH COMMUNITY

The fundamental principle upon which all aspects of the Reconstructionist program are based is the need to continue the adaptation of Judaism to meet the unprecedented circumstances of the contemporary era. That reconstruction applies not only to traditional Jewish beliefs and practices, but also to the very *structure* of Jewish communities.

Jews, who once were linked together across national boundaries by shared loyalty to halakhic authorities or talmudic academies, now require new mechanisms through which they can interact. Individual communities once were governed by Jewish law; in today's open societies, new communal forms must be developed. Synagogues of the past were part of autonomous, halakhically-governed communities in which rabbis were authorities. Today synagogues must function differently if they wish to serve Jews who live in secular society, and rabbis must learn to lead in the absence of any traditional authority. This chapter discusses the Reconstructionist approach to the reorganization of these Jewish institutions.

The Organic Jewish Community

From one perspective, all of the aspects of Mordecai Kaplan's program can be viewed as different dimensions of one grand concern: how the Jewish people might become one in spirit and reality. The political transformations of the modern world have created a situation in which Jews are divided not only by distances, but also by their widely divergent relationships to their governments. In the USA, with no established religion, Jewish denominations have been free to develop in their diversity and to attract Jews who voluntarily associate with them. In Israel, there is an established Orthodox rabbinate that exercises a virtual monopoly on religious practice. In France and England, there are Chief Rabbinates that function quite differently from those in such communist countries as the USSR and Rumania. Under such circumstances, Kaplan perceived a pressing need to develop an umbrella under which all Jewries and all committed Jews could be united.

Kaplan's understanding of religion led him, as discussed in chapter 3, to the insight that the primary way of expressing oneself as a Jew is to belong—to identify as a member of the Jewish people. He wanted to make that indefinite sense of belonging concrete, and he sought to develop a single governing apparatus through which the Jewish people could once again function as a whole.

Kaplan envisioned a democratically elected congress of representatives of the Jewish people that would create a constitution and government of individuals making a voluntary commitment. But once that commitment was made, the people's representatives would begin to struggle with defining what it means to be a Jew in our times. It would also provide an international basis for the Jewish people to help, support, and defend one another in times of crisis.

Of course, this reconstituted Jewish people would not define beliefs and practices. Kaplan firmly believed in the concept of unity, but unity within diversity. The key to the connection is belonging; believing and behaving are matters left up to smaller units of the Jewish people to define.

Jewish Centers

Kaplan sought to apply the same model to specific Jewish communities around the world. He deplored the competitive and antagonistic attitudes that Jewish institutions sometimes display towards one another. A goal of his proposed organic Jewish community was to put an end to such in-fighting.

Kaplan's plan was that in each neighborhood or area there would be one central Jewish address. Democratically elected officials would run the philanthropic, educational, religious, and social aspects of the community, collecting and using funds to benefit all. There would be a central staff of leaders representing all perspectives. People would be able to choose their preferred kind of worship service and education for their children, but they would all be housed under one roof. Even if people chose to worship in different services, they could still come together for an Oneg Shabbat, for example. Resources would be used more efficiently. There would be the advantage of an efficient body combined with the creativity of small, independent groups.

In this model, people would be brought together by what they share in common—their belonging to the Jewish community. Yet it would give them the freedom to express their Jewishness in a variety of ways.

Fifty years later, the vision described above remains only a vision. These ideas have had their impact, though. The Jewish center movement broadened synagogue commitments beyond religious services to include educational, social, and philanthropic concerns. The Federations in most cities have become central funding agencies for most nondenominational Jewish organizations concerned with the welfare of the Jewish community.

Yet these changes, while a vast improvement over the competitive and loose arrangements in Kaplan's time, are not yet "organic" in the sense he described. Federation boards are not democratically elected by all givers. This is not as serious a flaw from Kaplan's view as their primary failure—their inability to unite the religious and secular dimensions of Jewish life today. In essence, the synagogue has expanded its functions to include activities that parallel many supported by the secular establishments (fund-raising for Israel, adult education classes, gyms, philanthropic efforts on behalf of local poor, groups for older people), while Federations see themselves as the central address of the Jewish community and seek to develop quasi-religious commitments in the Jews involved in their efforts (Young Leadership programming and missions to Israel, for example). While a cooperative spirit often exists between synagogues and federations, the duplication of resources remains. The net effect is a sense that the secular and religious elements of the Jewish civilization do not fit together organically.

There is clear competition among the different religious groups, as well, and a lack of organicity exists there too. Though most local Boards of Rabbis draw the participation of Reform, Orthodox, Conservative, and Reconstructionist rabbis, they do not provide the unity Kaplan desired. And while we perceive that in some ways, the boundaries between groups have become less clear than in times past, institutional considerations still divide loyalties. Indeed, the rift between Orthodox and non-Orthodox is wider today—and growing, often fueled by political and organizational motives.

It is clear from the state of the Jewish community today that hopes for organicity are "utopian"; a desired goal perhaps, but impractical to realize. One might compare Kaplan's vision to that of the United Nations, where self-interest has overshadowed universalistic concerns. Like other dreams, the organic Jewish community stands out as an ideal, but one unlikely to be realized.

Reconstructionists today may derive a lesson from Kaplan's vision. We must maintain our own vision of the organic Jewish community, reconstructed for the next generation. Kaplan taught us that we should not only work for the Jewish people today, but must look ahead to the needs of the Jewish people tomorrow. Planning for the future means dreaming dreams, setting goals, and developing concrete plans for future generations of Jews. That means creative efforts to build for the future. We cannot abandon Kaplan's hope for an organic Jewish community; we must devote our efforts toward that end even if it is not realizable in our day. Indeed, if we believe that Judaism is a civilization—that belonging to the Jewish people is of utmost importance, that what draws us together as Jews is more basic than what divides us—then we can't abandon Kaplan's desire to express those ideas in practical terms.

The Reconstructionist Movement

In part, it was Kaplan's goal of Jewish unity that discouraged him from devoting most of his energy to the institutional establishment of the Reconstructionist movement. He sought instead to convince all Jewish groups of the veracity of his analysis of Jewish civilization and his program for the reconstruction of Jewish life. To that end, in 1940 he organized the Jewish Reconstructionist Foundation in New York. The Foundation served to publish his works and implement his program. Since then, many basic Reconstructionist ideas have been accepted by most non-Orthodox American Jews: the civilizational nature of Judaism, the primacy of belonging, the legitimacy of pluralism, the importance of ritual to nonhalakhic Jews, the synagogue as community center.

Another factor that inhibited the growth of the Reconstructionist movement through the 1950s was the anti-institutional bias of Reconstructionists. The other movements had developed unwieldy national organizations and large synagogues that were obstacles to the active involvement of individual Jews. Policy statements and halakhic rulings were issued from above, rendering individuals and congregations passive recipients. The American rabbinate developed a style of formality and authority that encouraged worshippers to become peripheral observers at services.

Eventually, however, Kaplan's followers overcame their reluctance to translate Reconstructionist ideas into institutional structures. They saw that they could not rely on other movements to implement the Reconstructionist program—a program needed to revitalize Judaism for disaffected, thinking Jews. That program required living communities. And so in 1954 the Federation of Reconstructionist Congregation and Havurot was formed, at first a group of only four congregations that grew to two dozen at the end of the 1970s and numbered just under sixty congregations and havurot in 1985.

Today, the FRCH coordinates the policies and activities of all Reconstructionist congregations and havurot. The FRCH staff provides consultation on such areas as by-laws and education, budgeting and liturgical innovation. Regional and national programs include lectures, workshops, retreats, intercongregational exchanges, an annual convention, youth programming, and policy statements. The Federation helps in the creation of new congregations, reaches out to unaffiliated groups, and conducts an ongoing program of public relations and outreach to unaffiliated individuals. It maintains the Reconstructionist Press and publishes the *Reconstructionist* magazine.

Reconstructionist Groups

Reconstructionist groups are characterized by their commitment to Judaism as a vehicle through which Jews find meaning in life. To that end, Reconstructionists are in a constant dialogue with the tradition, always searching the past for old ways and themselves for new ways of living Jewishly. For Judaism to be a means of self-fulfillment, Reconstructionists assert that it must touch one's whole being—intellectual and physical, spiritual and emotional. Therefore the exploration takes place both in *discussions* about a particular custom or value, and in *acting* on a custom or value.

For example, Jews universally recognize the importance of giving *tzedakah*. But from a Reconstructionist viewpoint, giving alone is not enough. The group must also study how the concept developed in Jewish history, what it meant to different Jewish communities in different places, what the values are which underlie giving as a commanded act, what the great rabbis and Jewish philosophers had to say about *tzedakah*. This is done in an attempt to understand what *tzedakah* is all about, and to empathize as much as possible with our ancestors. After learning about the Jewish tradition, the meaning of giving in secular Western culture is studied.

Ideally, in addition to studying together, the community collects *tzedakah* and decides—as a group—how to distribute the funds. This process also involves discussing the various places to send *tzedakah*: learning about the recipients, visiting them, making giving a personal act.

Committed to living in two civilizations, a Reconstructionist group gives to Jewish and secular causes alike. For example, many Reconstructionists have declared Halloween *Yom Yeladim* (Day of the Children) and have encouraged their children to "trick or treat" for UNICEF. They derive their pleasure from collecting funds for other children. This imbues the secular holiday with meaning and purpose, providing Jewish children with a unique way to live in two civilizations. By understanding the meaning of one's action, putting it into context, and learning and sharing the experience in a group setting, Judaism can lead simultaneously to fulfillment for the person's mind and spirit.

The Ḥavurah Idea

In order for this exploration to take place meaningfully, it must take place in a caring community. It is not surprising, therefore, that the ḥavurah idea first surfaced in Reconstructionist circles. The 1960 Reconstructionist convention in White Plains, New York, was devoted to the theme of ḥavurot. The following year the Reconstructionist Press published a pamphlet, *The Ḥavurah Idea*, written by Ira Eisenstein and Jacob Neusner. Ḥavurot in places like Denver, Colorado, and Whittier, California, have functioned continuously since then.

The Reconstructionist ḥavurah is a small group of people who are committed to uniting for their Jewish search. They worship, study, and celebrate holidays as an extended family. They struggle together through such issues as those we've described above. They share each other's joys and sorrows. These minicommunities create an intimate setting for learning and mutual support. To be sure, this attitude is dominant in Reconstructionist congregations as well. Some of these are structured as federations of ḥavurot and others follow a more traditional kind of synagogue model. The larger groups meet the need for intimacy by developing a variety of programs within the congregation which bring people together in subgroups.

The Shabbat seder is one such mechanism. It was Rabbi Kaplan who suggested that the best teaching tool in Jewish Life is the Pesaḥ seder. It would be appropriate for families on some Friday evenings, thought Kaplan, to conduct the Shabbat rituals, eat a festive meal, then ask and answer "Four Questions" on some Jewish theme. This alternative to late Friday evening services serves the purpose of bringing together small groups within the congregation for an intimate experience of celebration and study.

Another mechanism is the *hevrat mitzvah*—a group which is formed within a congregation with the express purpose of caring for any congregant in need. The *hevrat mitzvah* takes on such responsibilities as visiting the sick, helping families of sick or dying congregants with necessary chores, providing support for the unemployed and the newly divorced, and caring for the bereaved. Based on the traditional model of the *hevrah kadisha*—the holy society charged with caring for the dying and burial of the dead—the *hevrat mitzvah* cultivates a dimension of caring absent from much of congregational life. Many congregations divide the *hevrat mitzvah* into sub-groups to give special help where it is needed—to single-parent families, for example.

The emphasis on intimacy lends an informal air to Reconstructionist settings. Group singing, rather than choirs and organs, is the norm. The *shli'ah/shlihat tzibur* will as often play a guitar as lead the group *a cappella*. Group participation is paramount. Often members take turns leading services. The architecture of Reconstructionist buildings tends to support these efforts to maintain an air of informality. Sometimes Reconstructionist groups meet in someone's home, in a converted school building, or in facilities rented from a church or another synagogue. The aesthetic we strive for is not a sense of majesty and grandeur but one of intimacy and warmth. These elements lend a natural air to the life of the congregation or havurah. They also help us to remember that the building is a means to the end of Jewish community and not an end in itself.

The Participatory Process

Finally, Reconstructionist congregations and havurot and the Federation of these groups are run on the principles of democracy. Power and responsibility are shared among many. While Reconstructionist congregations may have typical board structures, membership on these boards is achieved through the contribution of work and wisdom more often than through wealth. All decisions, including decisions about ritual, are made in a democratic fashion.

Rather than passively receiving pronouncements from a committee of rabbis which dictates standards, Reconstructionist groups explore subjects requiring decisions on their own. Decisions like whether the synagogue should maintain the second day of two-day holidays, for example, or what rules for kashrut should be followed in the communal kitchen, are made in a way that involves the participation of the whole congregation. Members study the relevant Jewish texts, hear opinions on both sides of the issue, and then decide by reaching a compromise consensus—or by majority vote, where absolutely necessary. In a large congregation, this process begins in a committee, moves to the Board, and concludes with a congregational vote. In smaller groups, or with less important decisions, some of these steps are omitted. It is assumed that the process of sharing thoughts and feelings about an issue will sensitize the participants to the importance of that issue. While one conclusion sometimes seems obvious (we must keep a kosher kitchen so that any Jew can eat here), other factors arise when a discussion begins (what about members who don't keep kosher homes—how can they bring food into the community?), and a compromise may be reached which takes into account everyone's needs. Such a compromise might involve restricting the kitchen to dairy products. Alternately, the group might encourage *all* members to cook acceptable food in their own kitchens, whether those kitchens are kosher or not, to promote community sharing. Thus, observance can enrich the life of a synagogue without becoming an obstacle to Jewish renewal.

In such discussions, the rabbi has a unique perspective. As the person who has devoted his/her life to the study of the tradition and its vital interpretation, the rabbi may find that his/her orientation differs from the consensus of the group. In such situations, Reconstructionist rabbis do not insist that their communities conform to their own views, even as they retain their right to act in accordance with their own vision.

This kind of democratic process also takes place on the national scale. When the members of Reconstructionist congregations gather as a group, they share the kind of decision making that goes on in the congregations. During 1983–1984, the Federation of Reconstructionist Congregations and Ḥavurot (FRCH) was involved in formulating a resolution about intermarriage. Each group met to consider and suggest revisions of successive draft resolutions, and then delegates were designated to meet at the 1984 national convention in Buffalo. The final resolution—the result of much debate and compromise— thus reflected representatively the views of all groups and their members. In this way, the democratic *process* was as important—in the study and communication it engendered—as the ultimate wording. This is something that no rabbinical decision, rendered from above, could have achieved. (See Chapter 11 for information about obtaining the texts of FRCH resolutions.)

The Reconstructionist Magazine

Founded in 1935, the *Reconstructionist* is received by each member of all the Reconstructionist groups, as well as by many other subscribers. Its purpose is to facilitate the processes of learning and involvement that are at the heart of all Reconstructionist undertakings. The magazine runs editorials rooted in Jewish values and concerned with contemporary issues, thus assisting group discussions and activities that seek to bring a liberal Jewish perspective to bear upon contemporary issues. It offers programming ideas, reviews of recent books of Jewish interest, interpretations of ritual practices and traditional beliefs, surveys of Jewish cultural developments, introductions to fields of Jewish study, updates on issues relating to Jewish communities around the world, and help on problems facing congregations and havurot. In all of these ways, it assumes the intelligence and seriousness of its readers, as it attempts to provide Jews with the information they need to make intelligent choices about personal and global issues. Moreover, the magazine runs essays and symposia on topics that will be studied and discussed at national conventions, thus facilitating communication among Reconstructionists across the continent.

Pursuing a New Rabbinic Model

As should be apparent, Reconstructionist communities diverge substantially from the structure of most other congregations—primarily in their expressed and fervent commitment to participatory Judaism. The nature of liturgical and ritual observance is normally determined by group consensus after collective study. The leading of services, the reading of Torah, and the delivery of *divrei Torah* and sermons are rotated among capable members, while others study until they too are able. These communities are devoted to experimenting with traditional forms, based on the conviction that, as an evolving civilization of the Jewish people, Judaism will survive only if it is reconstructed to speak to the needs and in the idiom of contemporary Jews. Congregations are centers for Jewish culture and Jewish community.

For all of these reasons and others, when the time came to plan for the establishment of the Reconstructionist Rabbinical College (RRC), it was clear that such a school would need to train rabbis for new roles. Rabbis had to be educated to understand the evolving nature of Judaism, to serve Jews in a variety of new settings, and, most important, to become teachers and facilitators—leaders who would encourage their congregants to assume many of the roles and responsibilities that other American rabbis guard jealously as their own.

Rabbis no longer can function as halakhic authorities, since Reconstructionist Jews do not regard the halakhah as authoritative. In other non-Orthodox settings, rabbis have assumed the role of preacher—exhorting Jews to live up their ritual and ethical responsibilities—and of vicarious Jews—the model of Jewish observance and behavior for congregants who do not themselves choose to live observant Jewish lives.

These roles are unacceptable in a Reconstructionist setting. Instead, rabbis are trained to be teachers—Jews who have devoted years to the study of Jewish civilization so that they can serve as resource persons who can help others to learn about, understand, and empathize with Judaism and to grow into increasingly Judaized lives. Reconstructionist rabbis do not assume that solutions to complex issues can be found unambiguously within the Jewish tradition. Rather, they struggle with the dilemmas confronting contemporary Jews and attempt to help in resolving those dilemmas in ways that enrich their lives. Rather than perpetuating traditional liturgical and ritual forms regardless of congregants' understanding of them, Reconstructionist rabbis help Jews to understand the basis for traditional ritual, and to practice in meaningful ways—that turn out sometimes to be traditional and sometimes not.

The RRC Curriculum

Students who enter RRC (a bachelor's degree is required; many students already have prior graduate degrees or professional experience) study Judaism as an evolving religious civilization. Their course work is structured so that, in each year of the five-year program, the religion, language, law, literature, history, social organization, and culture of the Jewish people in a given era are presented. Students begin with a year concentrating on the biblical era (Abraham to Ezra), then study the rabbinic era (Babylonian exile to codification of the Talmud), medieval era (the founding of Islam to the Reformation), modern era (the discovery of America to the Holocaust), and conclude with the contemporary era (the founding of Israel to the present). Through the College's core civilization program, students develop a subtle awareness of the evolution of the Jewish people. In the middle of their program, students choose an area of concentrated study, thus developing a primary expertise in one area of Jewish learning.

The core civilization program is augmented by the requirement that students learn about other religions. RRC students develop an appreciation of living in two civilizations and an understanding of how the social scientific study of other religions and cultures can enhance their study of Judaism.

The third element of the RRC training program is required work in practical rabbinics. Through coordinated course work and field work, students develop the many skills needed in the rabbinate from counseling to administration, from education to community organizing. The goal of the practical program is to train rabbis to be facilitators within all settings in Jewish life—congregations, schools, and agencies. Because Judaism is a civilization, the rabbinic role should not be limited to the performance of religious functions only; rather, it should include teaching Jews to become more knowledgeable, whether at a Jewish "Y," day school, hospital, nursing home, counseling service, fundraising agency, or anywhere Jews seek to live Jewish lives. The development of new rabbinic roles does not replace the need for rabbis to function within congregations, and many RRC graduates choose to become congregational rabbis.

Rabbis in Reconstructionist Settings

How does the rabbi trained in the Reconstructionist mode participate in the congregation? The rabbi must see him/herself as a member of the congregation. The Reconstructionist rabbi is a person who struggles with conflicts, when they arise, between his or her own intuitions and the insights of the tradition, and looks for ways to have them work in harmony. The rabbi knows one can never completely work out the relationship between personal and professional priorities, but struggles with them honestly, openly, and with integrity. The Reconstructionist rabbi wants to help Jews assume as many of the rabbi's functions as possible—by teaching as many people as are willing to learn to do the things that he or she has learned to do. These are some of the qualities that the Reconstructionist Rabbinical College attempts to instill in its students.

As the process of rabbinic education involves more than classroom study and field work, much attention is given at RRC to building a learning community. Students and faculty attend retreats and seminars together to explore their own spiritual needs. Day-long colloquia and weekend programs have been devoted to the prevention of nuclear holocaust, feelings about sexuality, Jewish identity issues, God and prayer, Israeli-North American relations, death and dying, poverty, and mixing religion and political concerns. In addition, an active student body plays a decisive role in the discussion of curricular and administrative issues.

Reconstructionist Rabbinical Association

Graduates of the RRC are aware that their education does not end there. While they are learning from their congregants, they are expected to grow in their ability to teach them as well. To provide collegial support and a forum for discussing issues facing rabbis, the Reconstructionist Rabbinical Association (RRA) was founded in 1974. The RRA also includes graduates of other rabbinical institutions who feel an affinity with the Reconstructionist approach. All members join together in exploring issues at their annual meetings.

In its short history, the RRA has attempted to work out guidelines for dilemmas confronting the Reconstructionist community. Because personal status issues were in need of discussion, the rabbis first tackled conversion, divorce, and intermarriage. They work with fundamental Reconstructionist principles as they articulate these positions. Thus a thorough study of the traditional approach to each issue is presented. Then a document proposing needed reconstruction is drafted. The document is then discussed at length, as people with opposing points of view present opinions. In true Reconstructionist fashion, people listen to one another, and compromises are reached which truly give the past a vote, but not a veto.

On these issues, the RRA has supported egalitarian divorces and devised texts and ceremonies for them; supported the idea that a child raised as a Jew is Jewish if either parent is Jewish (traditionally, this could only be the mother); and suggested to rabbis that, while they should not perform Jewish wedding ceremonies for intermarrying couples, rabbis should be encouraging and supportive of the couples' efforts to maintain a Jewish home and communal affiliation.

These innovations come out of the Reconstructionist process just described. They are also most emphatically not a new halakhah. The RRA is conscious that it provides guidelines; rabbis are given the latitude to work with their communities to come up with guidelines of their own and to deviate from guidelines when conscience necessitates. The RRA is also aware that the guidelines it formulates are in need of almost constant revision and reconstruction; they are the beginning, not the end, of a process that needs to be carried on, augmented by the data of experience.

Having initiated its processes by dealing with personal status issues, the RRA has turned its attention to questions of professional and personal priorities, the role of family in Jewish life today, and issues in the area of biomedical ethics—the meaning of life and death, freedom and justice, sexuality and procreation.

As the FRCH turns its attention to issues of liturgical reform as well as to personal status questions and the future of Reconstructionism, the two groups will have much to teach and to learn from each other in the years to come. In keeping with the commitment to lay-rabbinic cooperation, joint commissions have been established to facilitate that process.

CHAPTER TEN

ENVISIONING THE FUTURE

It is the fate of our generation of North American Jews that many of us are *ba'alei teshuvah*—people returning to Judaism whose practice of and commitment to Judaism exceed those of our parents. A generation ago, our parents and grandparents struggled to Americanize; today, we struggle to be Jewish. The efforts of Eastern European Jewish immigrants and their children to shed their Jewishness have taken their toll. Our efforts to Judaize our lives are made with difficulty. The tradition and its forms often feel alien.

Nevertheless, our position as outsiders to the tradition also has its advantages. We are not Jews by inevitable momentum; for the most part, we do not practice Judaism because of an unarticulated nostalgia. Our commitments are made against the natural flow. They are self-motivated and authentic, filled with an energy and creativity that impel us to reconstruct the tradition to speak in the contemporary idiom.

Those of us who have returned by the Reconstructionist path find that the Jewish tradition is often exciting and enriching in ways that we could not have anticipated. Comfort with Jewish ritual comes only with practice—with an understanding of its meaning, but most importantly with the ease and naturalness that are earned by regular repetition. Whatever the lighting of the Shabbat candles, for example, is *supposed* to mean according to rabbis, philosophers, and mystics, its true meaning to an individual is discovered at the moment when the flickering of those candles and the resonance of the accompanying *berakhah* (blessing) make sense, signifying a real, internal transformation from workday concerns to the peace of the Shabbat. There are no shortcuts to that moment; it is earned by practice no less demanding than the meditation leading to Zen enlightenment, or the training that leads to the effortless swing of a master ballplayer. Judaism is a spiritual discipline.

Reconstructionist Jews have in common our acknowledgement that this Jewish mastery is as elusive as it is desirable. We struggle in the space between natural certainty and zealous skepticism. We share the quest to recover the beauty and power of the tradition without abandoning our commitment to modernity and intellectual integrity. As a result, our Jewish commitments inevitably are full of questioning and doubts. There are no easy answers.

Nevertheless, we pursue our Jewish commitments. There are rewards to be earned short of complete ease and mastery. In a depersonalizing, alienating, mobile society, a community of Jews seeking meaning is a priceless commodity. In a week devoted to the pressures of work, it is good to congregate in a common pursuit of the transcendent. In a world that often seems valueless at best and corrupting at worst, it is enriching to study and act on the basis of the values that past generations have designated as ultimate and sacred. In a late twentieth-century environment that tends to reduce everything to scientific utility and economic expediency, we find it imperative to ask the larger questions about the meaning of life. And as we do all these things, we find the Jewish tradition to be a particularly fertile field to seed our aspirations. Indeed, living with the threat of environmental disaster and nuclear holocaust, there is some comfort to be found in rediscovering a tradition that, in its timeless commitment to our struggle with *hubris*, activates us to behave in sane and life-saving ways. Beyond the excitement of technological advances, beyond the pleasures of fine wine and cheese and the thrill of professional success, the tradition is a vehicle for cultivating our essential common humanity. Through it, we can become better people.

And so we study our history, celebrate the cycle of the Jewish year, speak and contemplate the prayers of the tradition. We strive to transform Jewish civilization into a way of life through which we can become more fully human and more nearly divine. We seek the grounds of our ancestors' faith that this world is divinely created and inhabited, that God's presence within us and around us awaits our efforts to make it manifest. We are taking a double risk. We are deviating from accepted agnostic secular norms *and* from the traditional supernaturalism that demands a subservient, blind faith. We believe it is possible to be religious without being a fundamentalist, to be devoted to tradition without losing human sensitivity and intellectual openness, to be the beneficiaries of the past without becoming its slaves.

We do not pretend that any of this is easy. It is easier either to accept the tradition without question or to reject it entirely as outmoded, easier to accept an authority—whether the rabbi or the *New York Times*—than to reach independent conclusions. But as Reconstructionist Jews, we are comfortable with our questions and doubts. The process of admitting and confronting our uncertainty has itself become part of our norm. Our study of traditional texts is undertaken not so that we can accept them uncritically as true, but so that we can confront their meanings and wrest from them the part of their message that speaks to us. We sing our songs to recapture a celebratory state of consciousness and an attitude of gratefulness that we often find difficult to generate. We often pray and practice in the hope that we will understand afterwards what is unclear at the outset. We continue to do so because our frequent successes outweigh our inevitable failures.

In all of this, we believe that our approach to Jewish life speaks to many contemporary Jews who are seeking avenues of return to their Jewish identity. We like to think that we represent an adult Judaism for those who are willing and ready to confront the crisis of modernity. As adults, we acknowledge that most things in life are gray, not black or white. Our commitment to individual autonomy is at odds with the commanded, authoritarian nature of the tradition, but we are convinced that Jewish civilization is sufficiently resilient to be transformed successfully yet again, as it has evolved time and time again in our past. It is that faith that enables us to continue our struggle to reconstruct Judaism. That reconstructed Judaism is the necessary condition for Jewish vitality in our time.

CHAPTER ELEVEN

SUGGESTIONS FOR FURTHER EXPLORATION

This book is meant to be an introduction to the phenomenon of Reconstructionism, an invitation to further exploration. The suggestions for further reading below are organized to follow the sequence of chapters in the book.

THE RECONSTRUCTIONIST BOOKSHELF

The Best Place to Begin

Dynamic Judaism: The Essential Writings of Mordecai M. Kaplan, by Mel Scult and Emanuel Goldsmith (New York: Reconstructionist Press and Schocken Books, 1985). It includes extensive excerpts from Kaplan's works (both his books and less well-known writings) and general introductory essays on his life and thought.

Other Basic Introductions to Mordecai Kaplan's Life and Thought

Gilbert Rosenthal, *Four Paths to One God* (New York: Bloch Publishing Co., 1985), chapter 8; Kaplan's autobiographical statement, "The Way I Have Come" in *Mordecai M. Kaplan: An Evaluation,* Ira Eisenstein and Eugene Kohn, eds. (New York: The Jewish Reconstructionist Foundation, 1952); and Arthur Hertzberg, an introduction to *Judaism as a Civilization* (Philadelphia: The Jewish Publication Society and the Reconstructionist Press, 1981). For a concise introduction to Reconstructionism that is useful for teaching teenage students, see the Reform movement's magazine, *Keeping Posted* 27/3 (January 1982).

An Evolving Religious Civilization

For further discussions of "An Evolving Religious Civilization" (chapter 2 of this book), it is best to consult Kaplan's writings directly. See *Judaism as a Civilization* (1934), chapters 25 and 26, and *The Future of the American Jew* (1948) chapters 3 and 4. (All of Kaplan's works are available from the Reconstructionist Press. See the Resource Guide [next chapter] for information on how to order them.) Kaplan's concept of peoplehood has been explained clearly by Ira Eisenstein in *Judaism Under Freedom* (New York: Reconstructionist Press, 1956), chapter 4, and by Jack Cohen, "Peoplehood" in *Mordecai M. Kaplan: An Evaluation*. See also "The Spiritualization of Peoplehood and the Reconstructionist Curriculum of the Future" in *Creative Jewish Education: A Reconstructionist Perspective*, Jeffrey Schein and Jacob Staub, eds. (Rossel Books/Reconstructionist Rabbinical College Press, 1985).

The Concept of God

"The Concept of God" (chapter 3), is most clearly presented in Kaplan's *The Future of the American Jew*, chapters 10 and 14, and *The Meaning of God in Modern Jewish Religion* (1962). The latter is a magnificent study of the method of functional reinterpretation of the God idea as applied to the holiday cycle. A clear exposition of the issues is also available in Harold Kushner's *When Bad Things Happen to Good People* (New York: Schocken Books, 1981). Other important theological studies from a Reconstructionist perspective are David Brusin, "The God of Mordecai Kaplan," *Judaism* 29/2 (Spring 1980), pp. 209–220; Harold Kushner, "Why do the Righteous Suffer?" *Judaism* 28/3 (Summer 1970), pp. 316–323; Harold Schulweis, "From God to Godliness: A Proposal for a Predicate Theology," *Reconstructionist* 41/1 (February 1975), pp. 16–26. (See Resource Guide for information on how to subscribe to the *Reconstructionist* magazine.)

The Issue of Chosenness

To learn more about "The Issue of Chosenness," see Kaplan, *Future of the American Jew*, chapter 13; Richard Hirsh, et. al., "The Chosen People Reconsidered: A Symposium," *Reconstructionist* 50/1 (September 1984), pp. 8–28; and Arnold Eisen, *The Chosen People in America* (Bloomington: Indiana University Press, 1983).

Prayer and Ritual

The Reconstructionist approach to "prayer and ritual" is discussed in Kaplan's *The Future of the American Jew*, chapter 21. See also articles by Jacob Staub, "The Sabbath in Reconstructionism," *Judaism* 31/1 (Winter 1982), pp. 63–69; Rebecca T. Alpert, "The Reconstructionist Approach to Prayer: Some Questions and Answers," *Response* 13/1–2 (Fall–Winter 1982), pp. 127–131; Ruth F. Brin, "On Writing New Prayer Books," *Reconstructionist* 47/10 (February 1982), pp. 7–17; Robin C. Goldberg, "Seeing and Seeing Through:

Myth, Metaphor, and Meaning," *Reconstructionist* 50/7 (June 1985), pp. 9-14; Sidney Schwarz, "Beyond Responsive Readings," *Reconstructionist* 48/3 (May 1982), pp. 11-16. A symposium on Liturgy in Reconstructionism can be found in *Raayonot* 3/2 (Spring 1983). (*Raayonot* is available from the office of the Reconstructionist Rabbinical Association. See Resource Guide for information on how to contact the RRA.)

The Past Has a Vote, Not a Veto

To find out more about what is meant by "The Past Has a Vote, Not a Veto" (chapter 4 of this book), see Kaplan, *Judaism as a Civilization*, chapter 29, and *The Future of the American Jew*, chapter 19. Kaplan's explanation of transvaluation and revaluation is in *The Meaning of God in Modern Jewish Religion*, pp. 1-9. The Reconstructionist Rabbinical College Press (see Resource Guide) published a complete volume on Jewish Law in the series, *Jewish Civilization: Essays and Studies* Vol. 2, Ronald Brauner, ed., (Philadelphia, 1981). Of particular note are the studies by Mel Scult, Jacob Staub, Jack Cohen, Ira Eisenstein, and Richard Hirsh. A further development of decision making procedures is Rebecca Alpert's "Ethical Decision Making: A Reconstructionist Framework," *Reconstructionist* 50/7 (June 1985), pp. 15-20.

Living in Two Civilizations

The subject of "Living in Two Civilizations" (chapter 5) is approached by Kaplan in *The Religion of Ethical Nationhood* (1970), chapter 7. Further discussion of the subject is found in articles in the *Reconstructionist*: Nancy Fuchs-Kreimer, "The Thanksgiving Dilemma," 49/1 (October 1983), pp. 22-24; Daniel Nussbaum, "Two Civilizations or Three? Halloween as Yom Yeladim" 40/6 (October 1979), pp. 17-21; Jacob Staub, "Living in Two Civilizations: Preliminary Notes Towards a Reappraisal" 48/5 (Winter 1983), pp. 23-28; and Arthur Hertzberg, "Kaplan on the Promise of America," 50/3 (December 1984), pp. 13-16.

Interfaith Dialogue

On interfaith dialogue, see David Klatzker, "The 'Ecumenical' Kaplan," *Reconstructionist* 47/5 (July-August 1981), pp. 7-17 and volume 3 of *Jewish Civilization: Essays and Studies*, which is devoted to that subject.

Jewish Education

On the subject of Jewish Education, see *Creative Jewish Education: A Reconstructionist Perspective*, Jacob Staub and Jeffrey Schein, eds., (New York: Rossel Books and the RRC Press, 1985), especially the essay by Nancy Fuchs-Kreimer, "Teaching about Other Religions"; and Harold Kushner, *When Children Ask About God* (New York: Reconstructionist Press, 1971).

Public Policy Issues

On public policy issues, see the editorials in the *Reconstructionist* and the forum on the subject in *Raayonot* 3/1 (Winter 1983). Also see Rebecca T. Alpert, "Jewish Tradition and the Right to Health Care," *Reconstructionist* 49/6 (April–May 1984), pp. 15–20; Arthur Waskow, "Interpreting the Flood Story in the Nuclear Age," *Reconstructionist* 49/4 (February 1984), pp. 11–16; and Ira Chernus, "The Nuclear Issue: A Jewish Approach," *Reconstructionist* 50/8 (July–August 1985), pp. 7–9, 14.

Zion as a Spiritual Center

The Reconstructionist approach to "Zion as a Spiritual Center" (chapter 6) is presented by Kaplan in *The Future of the American Jew*, chapters 7 and 17, and *The Religion of Ethical Nationhood*, chapter 6. See also David Klatzker, "Renewing the New Zionism," *Reconstructionist* 50/5 (March 1985), pp. 10–14, and Jack J. Cohen, *The Case for Religious Naturalism* (New York: Jewish Reconstructionist Foundation, 1958), chapter 6.

Who is a Jew?

Discussions on the subject of "Who is a Jew" (chapter 7) are found in the "Symposium on Intermarriage" *Reconstructionist* 49/2–3 (November and December 1983), and in two articles on patrilineal descent: Richard Hirsh, "Jewish Identity and Patrilineal Descent: Some Second Thoughts" *Reconstructionist* 49/5 (March 1984), pp. 25–28, and Jacob Staub, "A Reconstructionist View on Patrilineal Descent," *Judaism* 34/1 (Winter 1985), pp. 97–106. The Reconstructionist Rabbinical Association's Guidelines on Conversion are available from the RRA (see Resource Guide). The Intermarriage Guidelines of the FRCH are in the newsletter insert within the *Reconstructionist* 50/1 (September 1985). For a lucid, scholarly survey on the history of matrilineal and patrilineal descent, see Shaye J.D.

Cohen, "The Matrilineal Principle in Historical Perspective," *Judaism* 34/1 (Winter 1985), pp. 9–13.

Women and Judaism

The original statement by Kaplan on "Women and Judaism" (chapter 8) is in *The Future of the American Jew*, chapter 20. Issues pertaining to women's roles have been discussed by Joy Levitt, "Woman Rabbis: a Pyrrhic Victory?," *Reconstructionist* 50/4 (Jan.–Feb. 1985), pp. 19–24; Sandy Eisenberg Sasso, "Women in the Rabbinate: A Personal Reflection," *Reconstructionist* 49/5 (March 1984), pp. 18–21; Rebecca T. Alpert, "Sisterhood is Ecumenical: Bridging the Gap Between Jewish and Christian Feminists," *Response* 16/2 (Spring 1984), pp. 3–16. "B'rit B'not Yisrael," is found in *Moment* (May–June 1975), pp. 50–51, and "Covenant of Washing" in *Menorah* 4/3–4 (April–May 1983), pp. 5–6.

Reorganizing the Jewish Community

Kaplan's view of "Reorganizing the Jewish Community" (chapter 9) is presented in *The Future of the American Jew*, chapter 6. On the ḥavurah, see Jacob Neusner, "Fellowship and the Crisis of Community," *Reconstructionist* 26/19 (January 1961), pp. 8–15, and Steven Stroiman, "A Practical Guide in the Formation of a Ḥavurah" in *Creative Jewish Education*, Schein and Staub, eds.

Training the Reconstructionist Rabbi

Rabbinic education from a Reconstructionist perspective has been treated by Rabbi Kaplan, *The Religion of Ethical Nationhood*, chapter 8; Ivan Caine, "Teaching Biblical Civilization" *Shiv'im: Essays and Studies in Honor of Ira Eisenstein*, ed. Ronald Brauner (Philadelphia and New York: RRC Press and KTAV Publishing House, 1977), pp. 3–14, and Rebecca Alpert, "The Making of a Rabbi: The Reconstructionist Approach," *Encyclopedia Judaica Yearbook* 1985.

Reconstructionist Congregational Life

On Reconstructionist congregational life, see Harriet A. Feiner, "The Synagogue as a Support System," *Reconstructionist* 50/4 (Jan.–Feb. 1985), pp. 25–30; Sidney Schwarz, "Reconstructionism as Process," *Reconstructionist* 45/4 (June 1979), pp. 14–18 and "A Synagogue with Principles," *Reconstructionist* 50/7 (June 1985), pp. 21–25; Arnold Rachlis, "The Aspirations of a Contemporary Rabbi," *Reconstructionist* 41/6 (September 1975), pp. 10–12; Harold Schulweis,

"Restructuring the Synagogue," *Conservative Judaism* 27/4 (Summer 1973), pp. 13–23; and the symposium on Lay-Rabbinic Relations, *Reconstructionist* 51/1 (September 1985).

The Future of Reconstructionism

For some further thoughts on the "Future of Reconstructionism" (chapter 10), see the symposium on the subject in *Raayonot* 2/1 (Winter 1982)/*Reconstructionist* 48/1 (March 1982), a symposium on "Neo-Hasidism and Reconstructionism," *Raayonot* 4/3 (Summer 1984), and Jacob Staub, "A Vision of Our Future," *Reconstructionist* 50/4 (Jan.–Feb. 1985), pp. 13–18. An important though somewhat dated study of the Reconstructionist movement itself is in Charles Liebman, *Aspects of the Religious Behavior of American Jews* (New York: KTAV Publishing Co., 1970), pp. 189–285.

THE RESOURCE GUIDE

For further information about the Reconstructionist movement, contact the following people and places:

Jewish Reconstructionist Foundation
Church Road and Greenwood Avenue
Wyncote PA 19095, Phone: 215 887-1988

The Reconstructionist movement operates through a membership body, organized in 1940, known as the Jewish Reconstructionist Foundation. Membership, which includes a subscription to the *Reconstructionist* magazine, is $50 per year. Write to the JRF for information about membership.

The Federation of Reconstructionist Congregations and Havurot
Church Road and Greenwood Avenue
Wyncote PA 19095, Phone: 215 887-1988

Founded in 1954, the Federation of Reconstructionist Congregations and Ḥavurot coordinates the policies and activities of all the Reconstructionist congregations and ḥavurot. Growing at a rate of about 20% each year, the FRCH extends from Montreal to Curaçao and from New York to California.

In serving the needs of existing congregations and ḥavurot, the

FRCH staff provides consultation on areas as diverse as by-laws and education, budgeting and liturgical innovation. It also helps with arranging lectures and scholars-in-residence on themes reflecting the Reconstructionist approach. Through visitation, the staff also provides workshops and on-site training.

Regional and national programs include lectures, workshops, retreats, intercongregational exchanges, an annual convention, youth programming, and policy statements.

The Federation helps in the creation of new congregations, reaches out to unaffiliated groups, and conducts an ongoing program of public relations and outreach to unaffiliated individuals to increase awareness of Reconstructionism.

A relatively young organization, the FRCH is putting substantial energy into expanding its programs, which soon will include family camps, a full network of regional offices, expanded educational and youth services, and an Israel office and program.

If you wish to become more involved, or to organize a congregation or havurah, write the FRCH.

The Reconstructionist Magazine
Church Road and Greenwood Avenue
Wyncote PA 19095, Phone: 215 887-1988

The *Reconstructionist* addresses religious, political, social, and moral issues of contemporary Jewish life; explores modes of spiritual growth for the individual Jew and for Jewish communities; and reviews the significance of Jewish civilization in all of its facets, past and present. It strives to be innovative, and, when necessary, controversial. Thus, the *Reconstructionist* serves as a medium for the continuing development of Reconstructionist ideas, practices, and institutions. The magazine is published by *The Federation of Reconstructionist Congregations and Havurot.* Subscriptions cost $20 per year; foreign, $3 extra; single copies, $3.

The Reconstructionist Press
Church Road and Greenwood Avenue
Wyncote PA 19095, Phone: 215 887-1988

Many of the titles listed in the Reconstructionist Bookshelf are available from the Reconstructionist Press, which has published more than fifty titles including nonfiction, pamphlets, prayerbooks, syllabi, cantatas, and poetry. A booklist is available from the FRCH upon request.

The Reconstructionist Rabbinical College
Church Road and Greenwood Avenue
Wyncote PA 19095, Phone: 215 576-0800

The RRC is a community of teachers and students dedicated to the renewal of the rabbinate in the North American Jewish community. It offers a five-year graduate program leading to rabbinical ordination and the Master of Arts in Hebrew Letters. The College prepares men and women for leadership and service in every aspect of Jewish communal life. The Reconstructionist rabbi may serve in a synagogue, teach in a university, act as a resource person for a network of havurot, work with a federation or welfare fund, direct a Hillel foundation, head a bureau of Jewish education, administer a Jewish center, or staff a Jewish communal agency.

At RRC, Judaism is studied and experienced as the evolving religious civilization of the Jewish people. Students concentrate each year on a specific period of Jewish history—biblical, rabbinic, medieval, modern, and contemporary—through a series of courses dealing with the history, thought, and classical literature of each era. Preparation for the practical rabbinate is offered through courses in pastoral counseling, education, and other rabbinic skills. In the final two years of the program, students declare a major area of study and take advanced courses in that area, enabling them to prepare in depth those areas of Judaica which they see as central to their own rabbinate.

In keeping with the conviction that rabbis need to have a firm understanding of the world in which they serve, the RRC curriculum includes required study in world religions, the social sciences, and philosophy, emphasizing those areas in each field which have interacted with and influenced Judaism throughout its historical development.

In the Philadelphia Jewish community, students gain professional experience and fulfill community service requirements through supervised in-service training in synagogues, agencies, and schools.

Reconstructionist Rabbinical Association
Church Road and Greenwood Avenue
Wyncote PA 19095, Phone: 215 576-0800

The RRA is composed of graduates of the RRC as well as graduates of other rabbinical institutions who choose to identify with Reconstructionist Judaism. In addition to working in the areas of ritual, liturgy, education, and youth, the RRA has a *bet din* (religious court), as well as special commissions on marriage and divorce, intermarriage, and other areas. The RRA also serves as the professional organization of its members, dealing with placement, contracts, and insurance. For information about membership or to receive copies of RRA guidelines, contact: the RRA.

Raayonot
Church Road and Greenwood Avenue
Wyncote PA 19095, Phone: 215 576-0800

Raayonot is the rabbinical journal published by the Reconstructionist Rabbinical Association. Back copies of issues mentioned in the Reconstructionist Bookshelf are available in limited quantities for $3 from the RRA.

The Shalom Center
7318 Germantown Avenue
Philadelphia PA 19119, Phone: 215 576-0800

In early 1984, the Reconstructionist Rabbinical College took the initiative to bring into being the Shalom Center, a broad-based national resource center for Jewish perspectives on preventing a nuclear holocaust. The Shalom Center has its own board, on which sit leading rabbis of all four religious movements and leaders of a number of secular and communal Jewish organizations. One of the Shalom Center's main concerns is the reinterpretation of Torah to understand how to respond to the danger of nuclear holocaust. Members receive *The Shalom Report* every two months, as well as sermons, curricula, liturgies, and position papers.